MONSTER
THIS BOOK
BELONGS TO
Luka

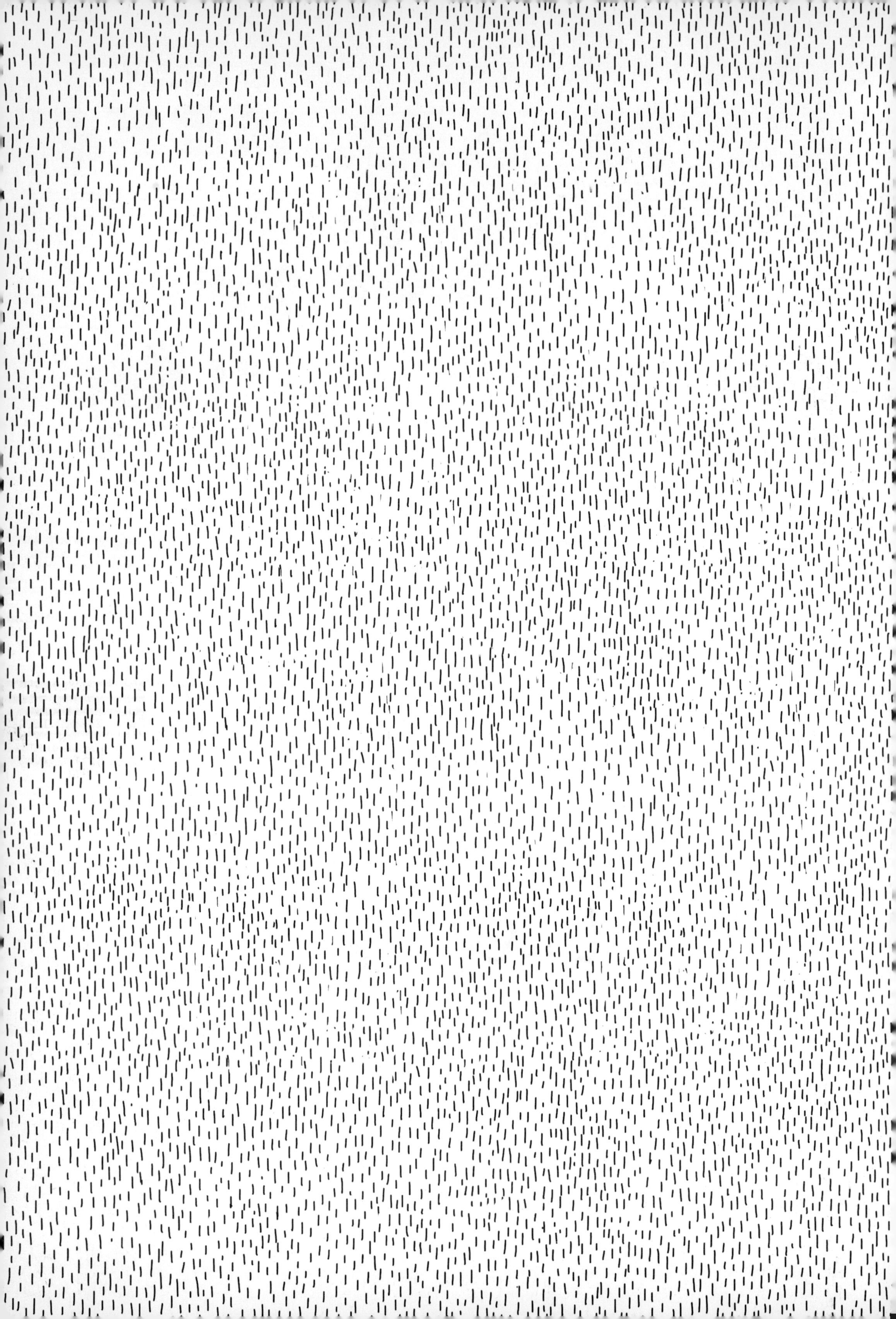

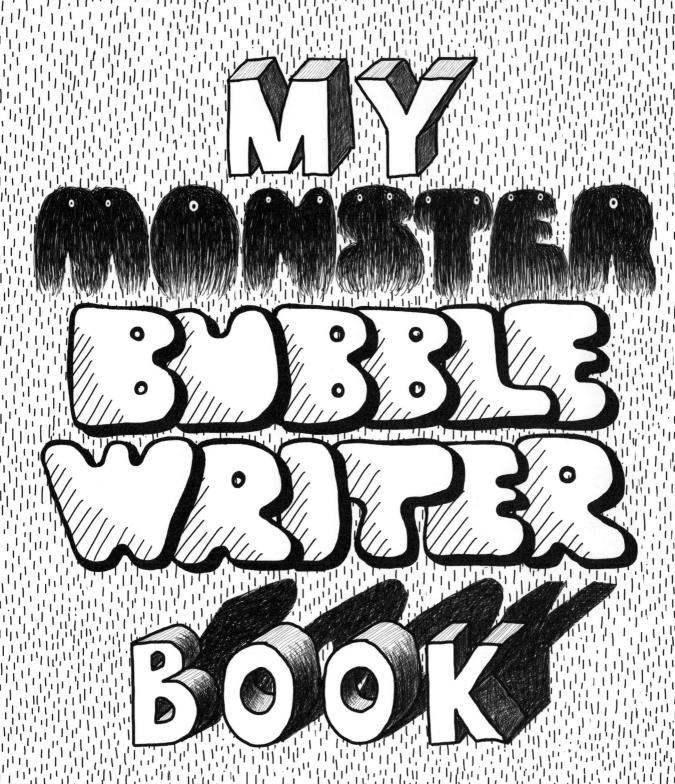

MY MONSTER BUBBLE WRITER BOOK

THIS BOOK IS ALL ABOUT MONSTERS, BUBBLE WRITING, AND DRAWING – THREE OF THE BEST THINGS IN THE WORLD! WHAT'S NOT TO LOVE?

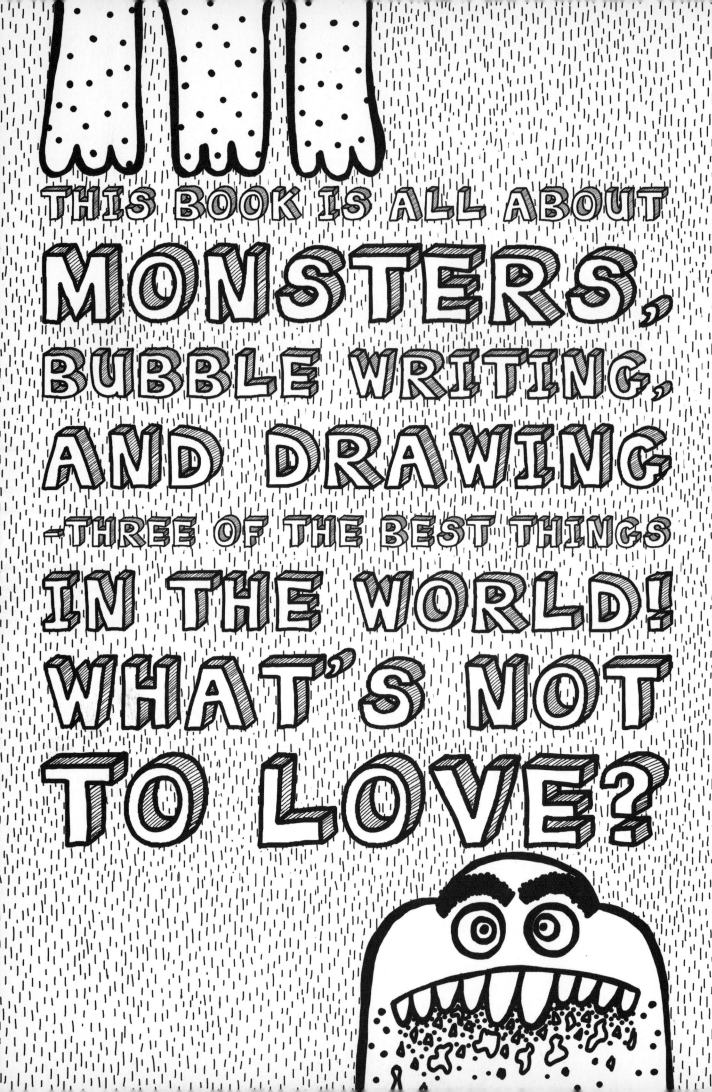

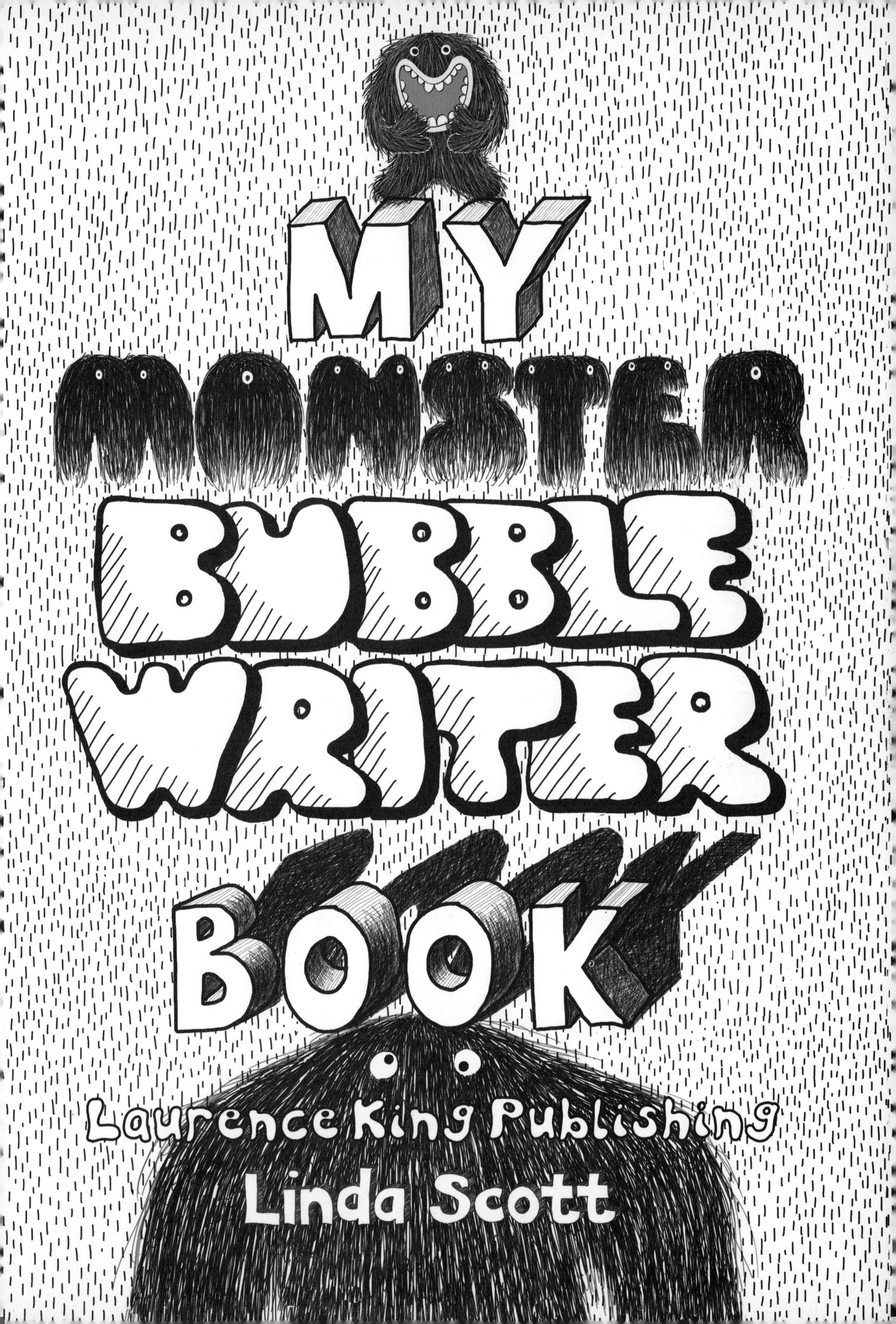
MY
MONSTER
BUBBLE
WRITER
BOOK
Laurence King Publishing
Linda Scott

hello

Published in 2013 by
Laurence King Publishing Ltd
361-373 City Road
London EC1V 1LR
United Kingdom

Tel: +44 20 7841 6900
Fax: +44 20 7841 6910
e-mail: enquiries@laurenceking.com
www.laurenceking.com

A catalogue record for this book is available from the British Library

ISBN: 978-1-78067-102-4

The publisher is grateful for permission to reprint from the following copyright material by Roald Dahl:
Revolting Rhymes (page 116 top and page 117 bottom) and The BFG (page 116 middle and page 117 top) courtesy Jonathan Cape Ltd and Penguin Books Ltd; James and the Giant Peach (page 116 bottom) and The Magic Finger (page 117 middle) courtesy Penguin Books Ltd.

Commissioning Editor: Helen Rochester
Design: Mark Holt
Printed in China

Contents

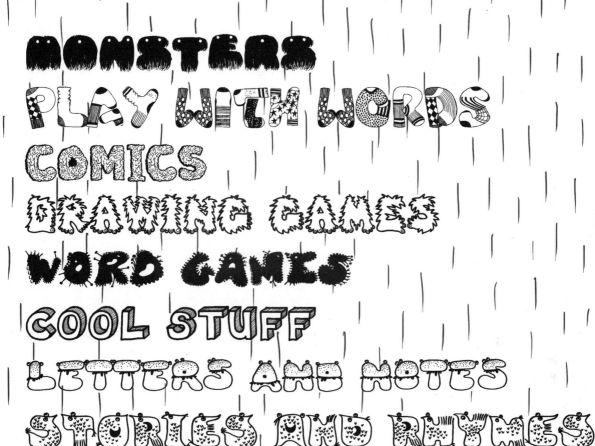

What's the big deal about bubble writing and drawing monsters?

Well, if anyone knows me then you already know that I consider bubble writing the absolute best thing in the entire world. I love all forms of writing and communicating but bubble writing will always be top of the list for me!
If you don't have a clue about what bubble writing is, well it's hand-drawn letters that can look quite 'bubbly' in their original form but can be developed into lots of interesting, creative styles.

And monsters? It's just so cool to be able to draw monsters, and it's even better to create your own monsters from your imagination!

When you throw bubble writing and monsters together, WOW! It's like an explosion of bonkers creativity! In this book you will see that monster alphabets are some of the most wonderful bubble writing alphabets out there. Hopefully with all of this inspiration at your fingertips you will create some glorious ones yourself! If you do - then please share them with me at: **www.facebook.com/thebubblewriter.**

Above having fun with monsters, this book is about COMMUNICATING WITH WORDS: Letters, notes, games, riddles, messages, memos, and more. Writing is so important and HAVING FUN while you do it is even more so. So GET WRITING, HAVE FUN, AND BE HAPPY. The Bubble Writer

Let's take a look at two of the basic alphabet styles to master first. Once you know your way around these two then most bubble writing challenges will come easy!

First, **Basic Outline**:

Write your name in pencil in your neatest handwriting. Try to make the letters all the same size and shape (use graph paper if it helps!). Next, draw an outline around the letters in pencil. When you are happy, go over in pen.

Next comes **Freehand**:

The same principles apply for this alphabet but this time write in your natural handwriting – including wonky bits, crazy curves and all!

Of course, the above are just the basics for mastering both these alphabets. Once you've got the basics licked, then it's time to go wild!

Now turn over the page and GO FOR IT!

The Bubble Writer

To create the most interesting fonts you need to be able to do a basic outline with your eyes closed...

Basic Outline

"Aa Bb Cc Dd Ee Ff Gg
Hh Ii Jj Kk Ll Mm Nn
Oo Pp Qq Rr Ss Tt Uu
Vv Ww Xx Yy Zz !?"

Once you know how to write in freehand style then you can manage all the curvy type of fonts...

freehand

!abcde"fghi jklmnopqr stuv,,wxyz?

Hello Super Furry Dude

Practice The Dude's letters here...

Say what???

"ABCDEFGHIJ
KLMNOPQR!?
STUVWXYZ"

LET'S
MAKE
SOME
MONSTERS
He's such a dude, dude!

In this section I will show you how to make your own monsters. You can take inspiration from all around you to make your monsters: Look at your friends, teachers, enemies, and heroes and just let your imagination go crazy. Remember - there's no such thing as a monster that's 'wrong'! So enjoy yourself and if you can - try to draw a monster every day!

The Dude knows some spooky
little monsters
Color them in . . .

You can use these features to help...

...make these shapes into your own monsters

WHAT A CRAZY LOOKING MONSTER!

CAN YOU MAKE THIS FELLA LOOK DIFFERENT?

Here are some friendly little monster dudes

Give them some cool t-shirts and patterns

MAKE a Monster
IN THE BLANK SPACE
...Dude!
Hey Man
Be inspired by a ballpoint!!
Make it crazy!

Weee!
Argh! The dreaded Hand Monster
CAN YOU make one TOO?

Big foot monsters

What do these stinkers look like?

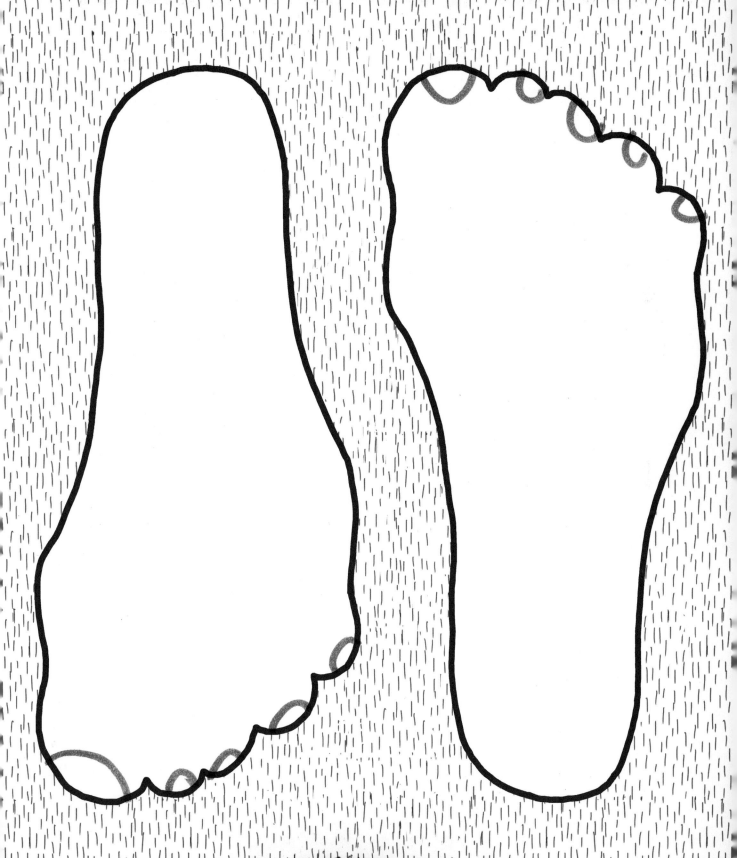

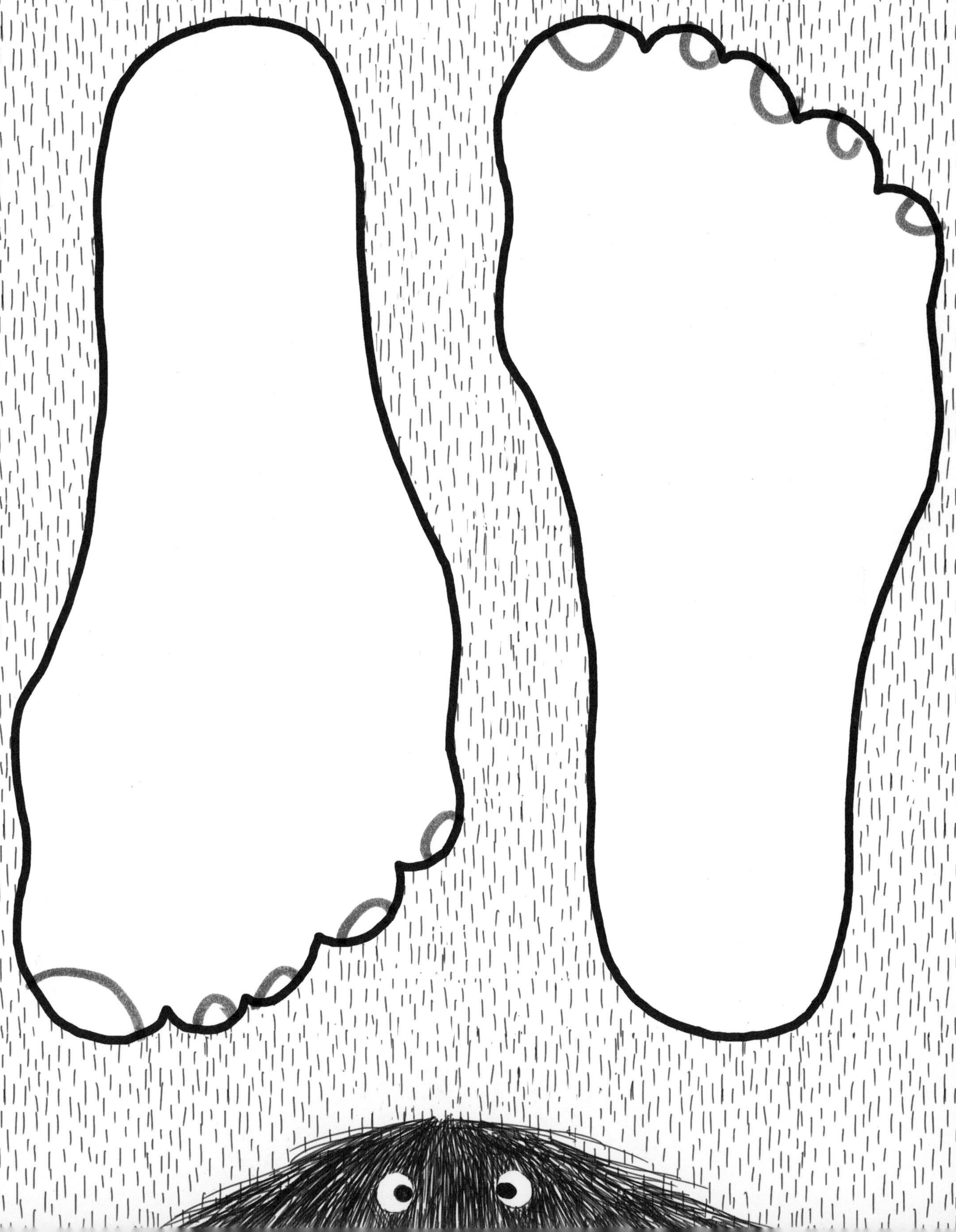

MAKE SOME SCARY MONSTERS HERE

AND SOME FRIENDLY MONSTERS HERE

OH HI THERE

SOCK MONSTER

(HE EATS YOUR SOCKS ONE AT A TIME)

Practice your sock letters here

"ABCDEFGHI"
JKLMNOPQR
STUVWXYZ!?

Let's play with words
All right Socky, calm down!

I am going to help you with your bubble writing skills by showing you how to play with words: You can mess around with your verbs, nouns, and adjectives...heck, drawing words to look like their meaning is pretty much the most fun in the world! This, and then making your words 3D by adding shadow and perspective will make you a super - advanced bubble writer!

How about some weather words?

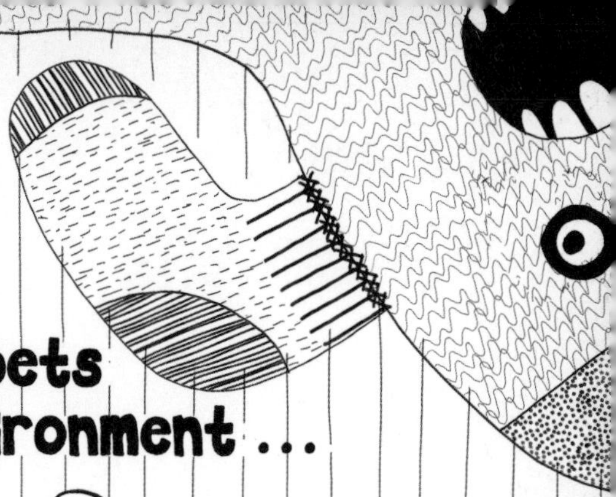

Socky loves to make words and alphabets that look like the weather or the environment ...

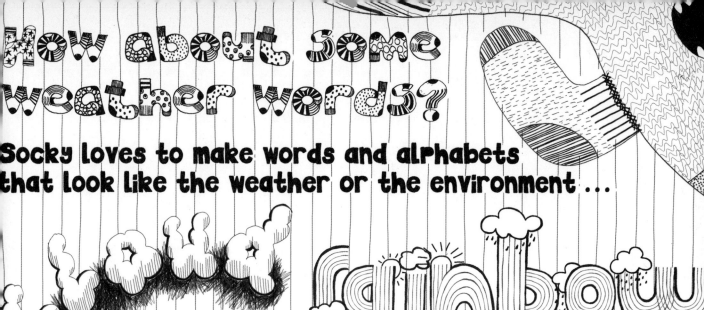

cloud rainbow

LIGHTNING HOT

How about trying these?

COLD . WIND . STORM . ROCK . SEA
FOREST . STARS . DESERT . GRASS

BRING ON THE VERBS
These words look like what they mean...
Stretch
Fall
POP
SMILE
PUNCH
CRASH
MELT
DRIP
bounce

Now you draw some verbs

Socky says, 'Try these'

HOP . SCREAM . BLOW . KICK . LOOK
SHAKE . FREEZE . SQUASH . LAUGH

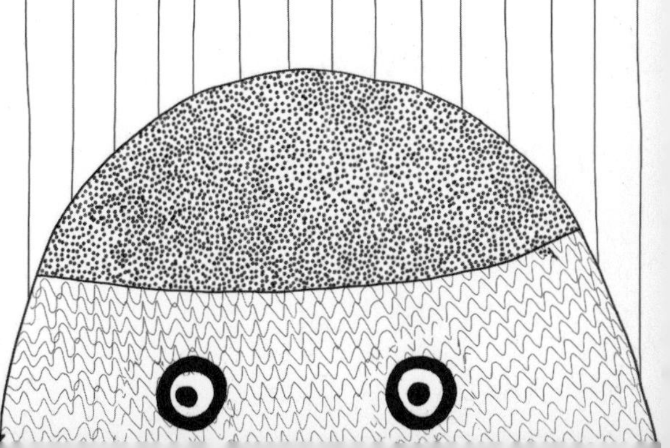

LET'S THROW SOME NOUNS AROUND

These words mean what they say...

How about some nouns now?

Socky says, 'Have a go with these words'

TREES . BONES . BALLOONS . RULER

WOOD . HILLS . SCARS . RAINBOWS

WELL HELLO ADJECTIVES

These words really say it all...

SLIMY

hairy

STRIPY

FAT

SHAKY

Spooky

ITCHY

BRUISED

You know what to do

Socky says, 'Have a go at these'

SPOTTY . MUDDY . SCARED . FURRY
FOGGY . SWEATY . TALL . CRACKED

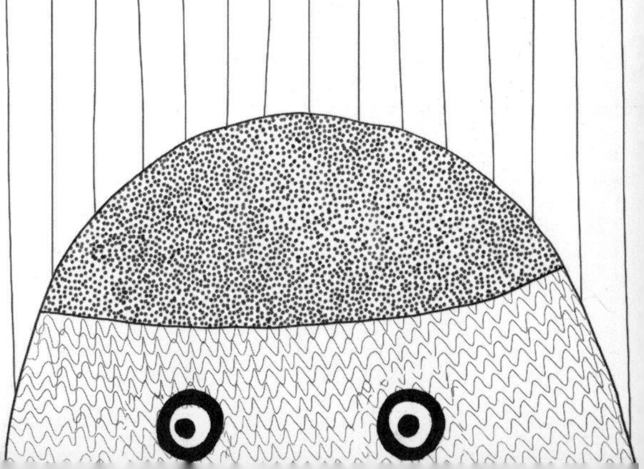

WORD SHAPES

These are great for messages, posters, and banners

MAKE A SHAPE TO PUT YOUR MESSAGE IN.

What would you like to say to Socky?

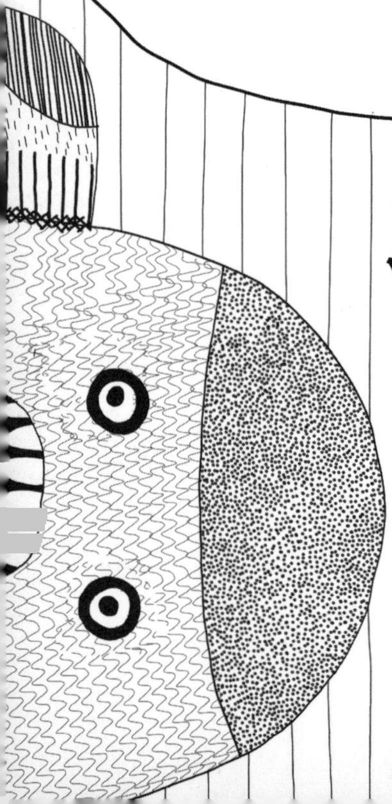

WORD SHAPES

Practice writing in the shapes!

You get the idea...

MAKING THINGS INTERESTING

Take notice of perspective, shadow, and 3D to really take your words to a totally bonkers level!

MONSTER

MONSTER

MONSTER

MONSTER

MONSTER

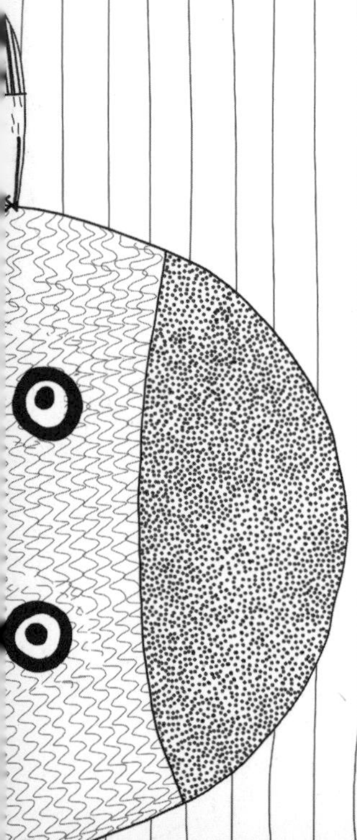

Try some 3D and shadow effects here...

SUPER HEROES

Make Socky a cool **super hero** name for his costume...

MONSTER

MONSTER

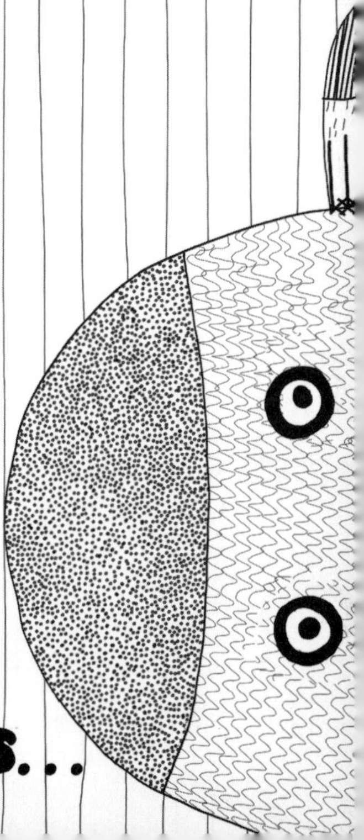

Now try some perspective 'super hero' words...

Introducing...

gooey brain monster

Practice the brain monster letters here

" a b c d e f g h i j

k l m n o p q r s ; ,

t u v w x y z ! ?

Let's make some
Comics

Once you know how to draw monsters and do cool bubble writing then a great way to combine the two is by making comics. Get hold of any kind of sketchbook and keep it just for your comic ideas and finished comic strips. Draw a monster character then give it lots of different adventures. Your own comic - creating adventure starts here!

Comic speech bubbles

You can use these in your comic stories

Write some cool bubble words and thoughts inside

A page of smiles!

You can make your monsters and characters look so different by changing their mouths...

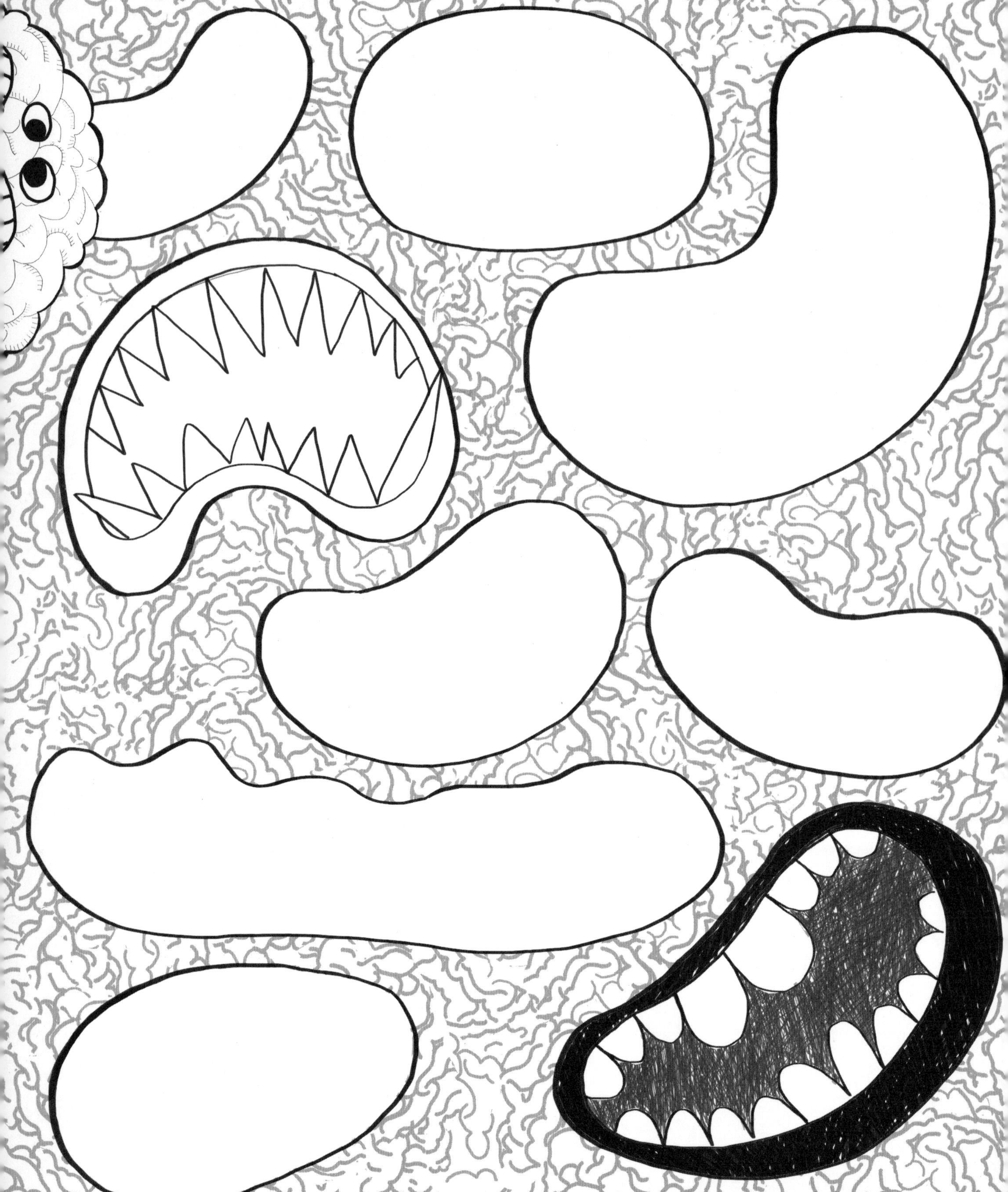

(They can be sneers and snarls too)

Comic-style action words

Comic stories are full of real action so you'll need some dramatic words to help them along

WOW
kerrrrrbang!
(is this even a word?)
Aaaaarrrggghhhhhh

Make some more

Finish this comic strip

You can make it happy or sad, funny or sour and give him somewhere super-cool to live!

THE END

WHAT IS THIS MONSTER SAYING TO YOU?
Try and use letters that look LIKE HIM

NOW LET'S MAKE HIM A COMIC STRIP

START WITH PENCIL THEN GRAB A BALLPOINT AND YOUR COLORS LATER

THE END

NOW MAKE A COMIC ABOUT GOOEY

surprise!
THE END

Hey man! It's the...

WEIRDY BEARDY GUY

Don't be fooled by those sandals...he's mean!

Practice, practice, practice!

ABCDEFGHIJ

KLMNOPQRS

TUVWXYZ!?

LET'S PLAY DRAWING GAMES

Drawing games have been around for as long as the hills. Here's a couple in this section but really all you need is a friend, some paper, a couple of pencils, and a great imagination. Have fun!

I AM AN EXQUISITE CORPSE
MY NAME IS

Give this crazy creature a crazy name!

Make a friendly exquisite corpse here

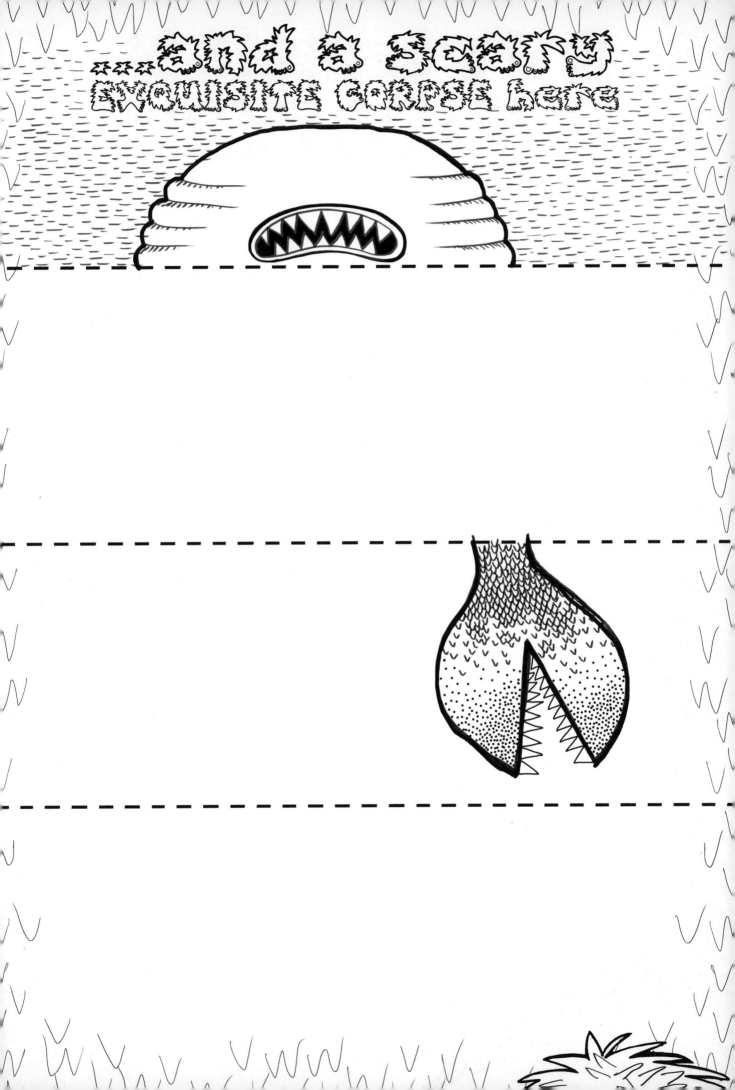

…and a scary exquisite corpse here

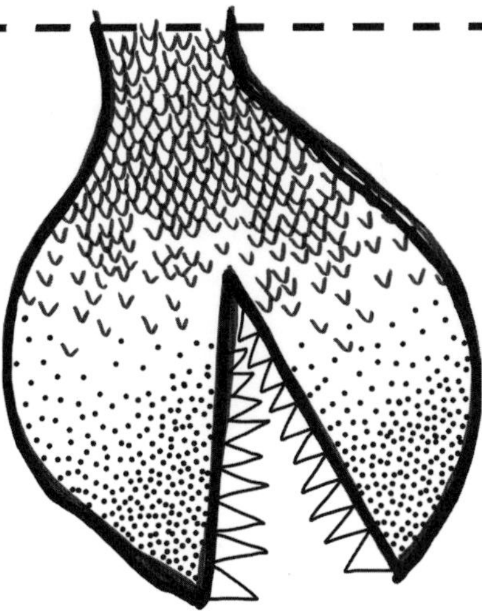

A friendly exquisite corpse

Find a friend and create a monster together

A deadly exquisite corpse

How deadly looking can you make this monster?

MONSTERDOKU!

this one is easy!

MONSTERDOKU!

1 2 3 4 5 6 7 8 9

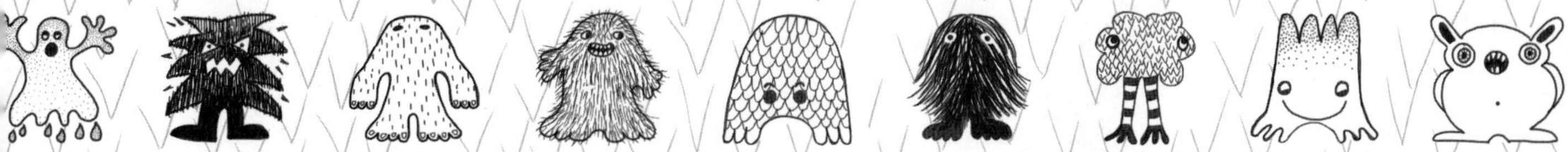

This one is hard!

Monster doodle game...
turn the doodle into a monster (or a bear!)

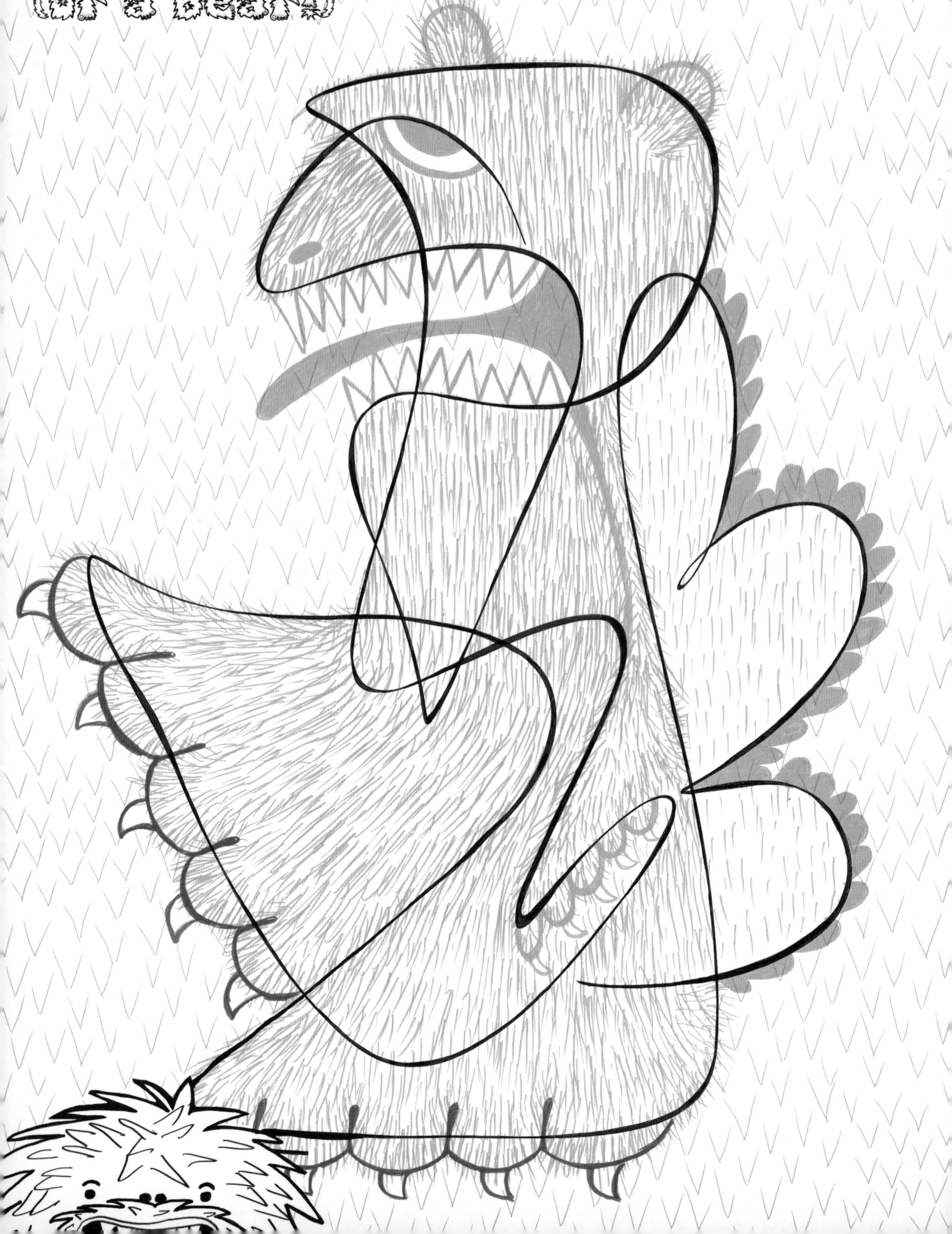

Can you make this one look really different?

DRAW A MONSTER

FRIEND FOR BEARDY

DRAW ANOTHER MONSTER!

Well hello there crazy...

Germ bugs

Wow, they make your skin itch!

Practice some germ letters here...

"abcdefghi"

jklmnopqrs

tuvwxyz!?

Let's Play Word Games!

In this section we will show you some word games. Playing with words and especially bubble writing is the most creative and brilliant way to spend your time EVER! Make your own alphabets, codes, monster words, and letters then share them with your friends and start communicating together in a language that only you can understand!

Make your own monster alphabet

What sort of hair does it have? Does it have horns? What about claws? Is it evil or friendly? Give it a mouth and eyes...

Start with these freestyle letters

A B C D E F G

H I J K L M N

O P Q R S T U

V W X Y Z ! ?

Here's a monster secret code

Now work this out!

Have a go at making your own monster secret code!

A B C D E F G

H I J K L M N

O P Q R S T U

V W X Y Z ! ?

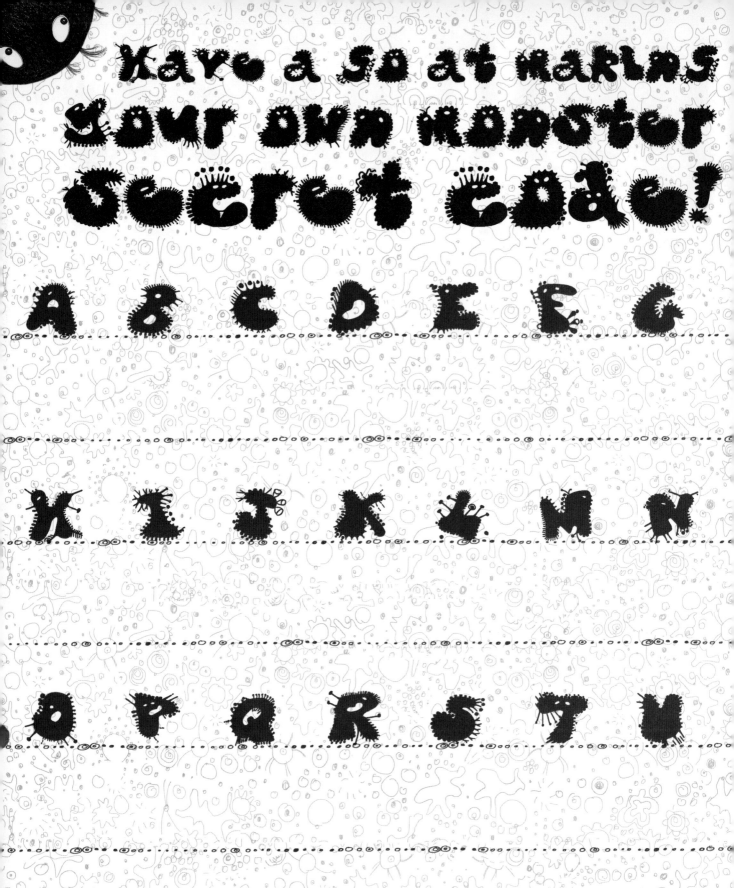

Write something truly amazing about yourself! (In code)

SPEECH BUBBLES

You can be inspired by absolutely everything around you to make exciting letters and words.

Can you finish this alphabet?

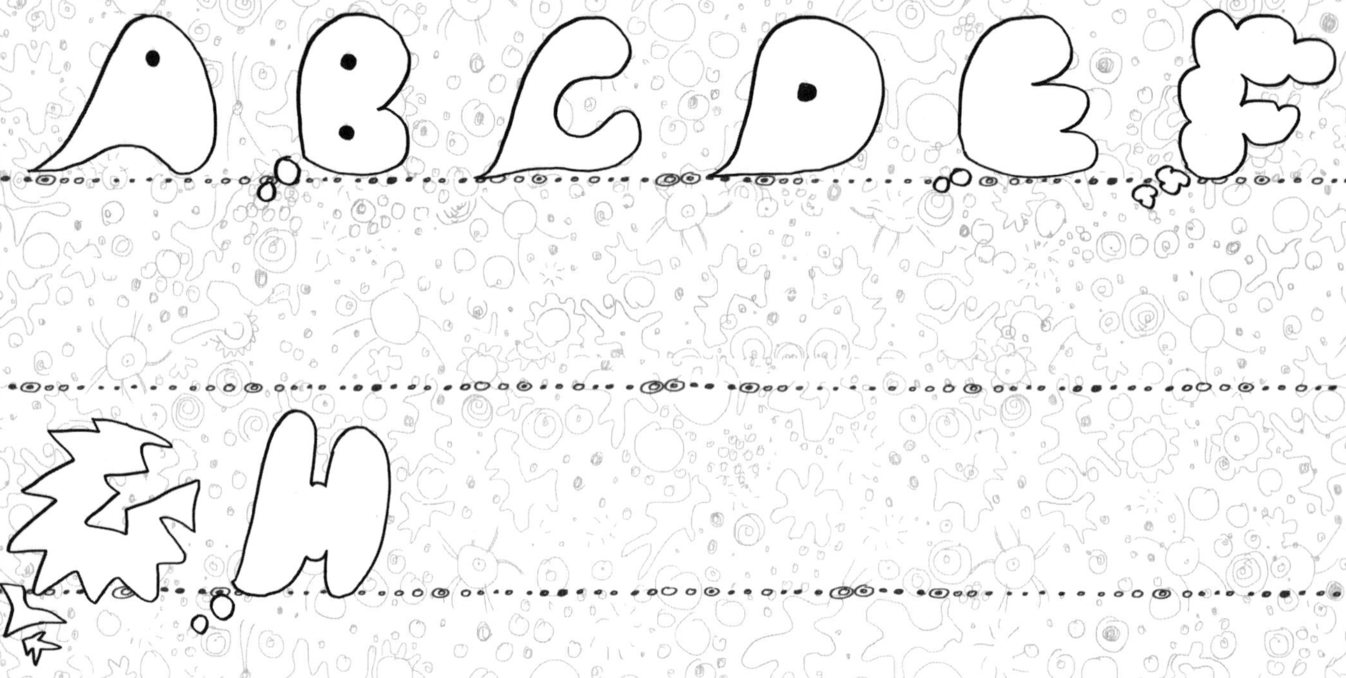

This alphabet would be great to use on your comic pages!

FLOATING LANDS

I have no idea where on earth the inspiration came for these letters! Where do you think?

Can you finish this alphabet?

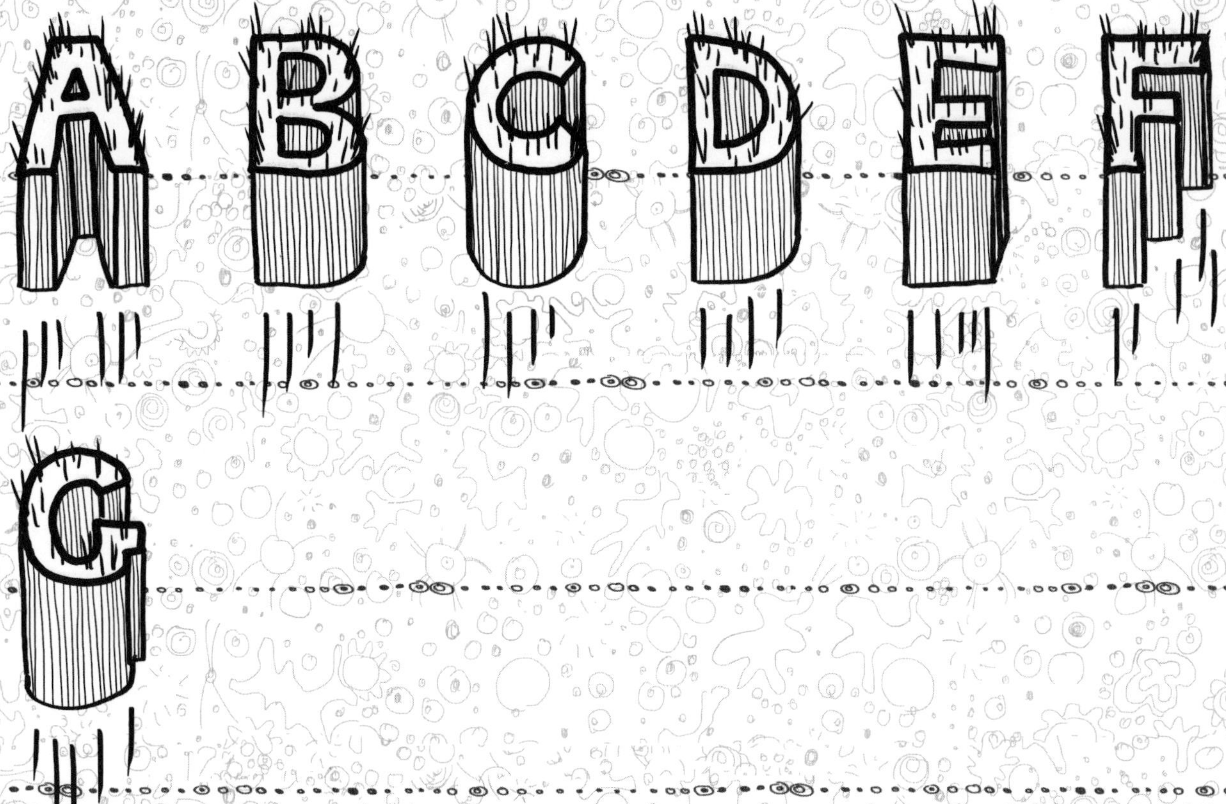

MONSTER NAMES

These monster names look just like the monsters themselves!

hair monster

It's this guy that makes your hair look bad!

You didn't really think there was a fairy did you?

TOOTH MONSTER

dirt monster

Now THIS fella gets EVERY-WHERE!

Now You Make Some Cool Monster Words

Try these:

Shoe Monster

Lazy Monster

Money Monster

Germbug's Monster Wordsearch

scared
teeth
bite
googly
eyes

gobble
freaky
monster
bogeyman
claws

hairy
fierce
furry
gross
slime

gore
hide
roar
scream
badbreath

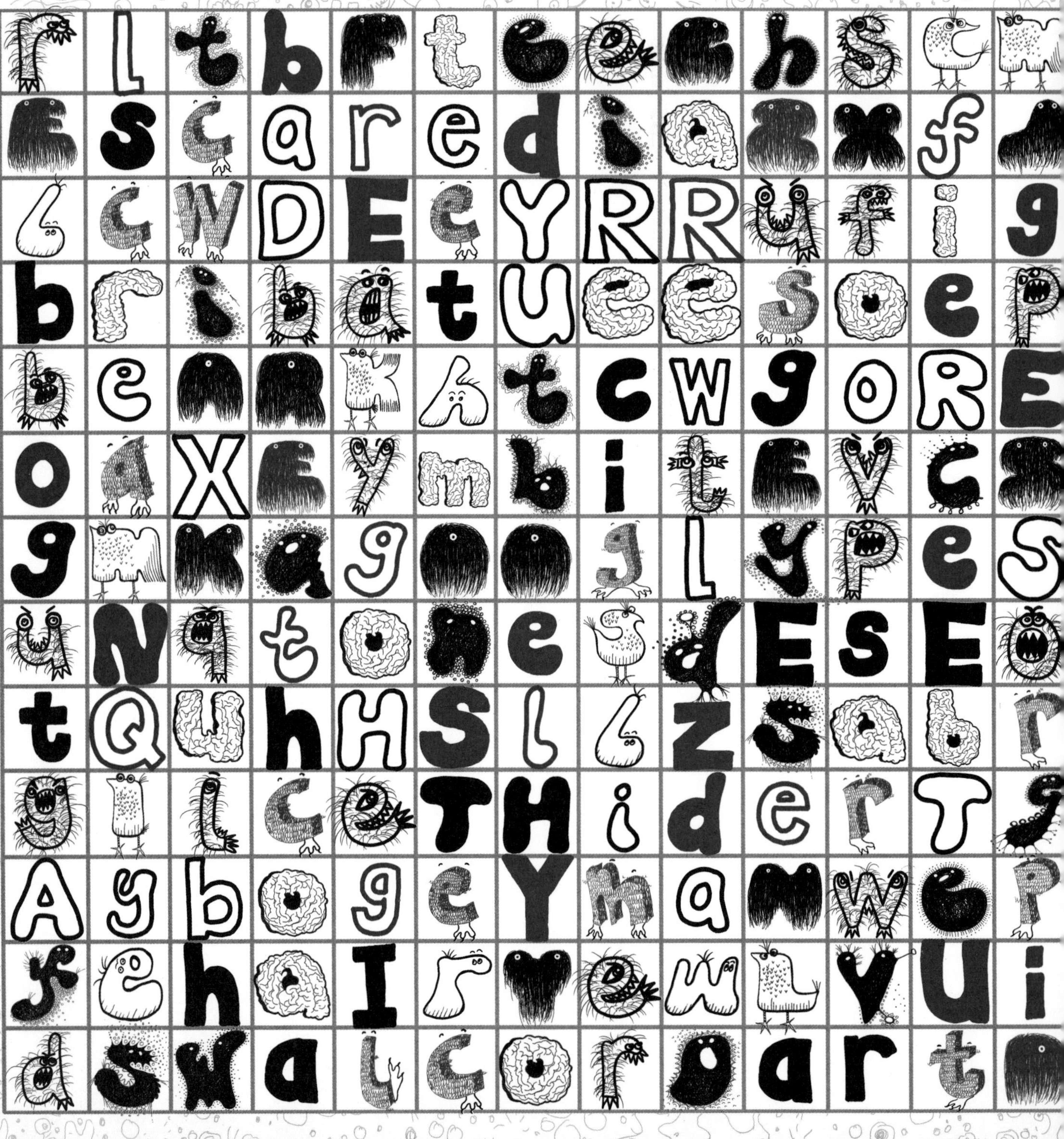

DIY Wordsearch

Make your own and have some fun

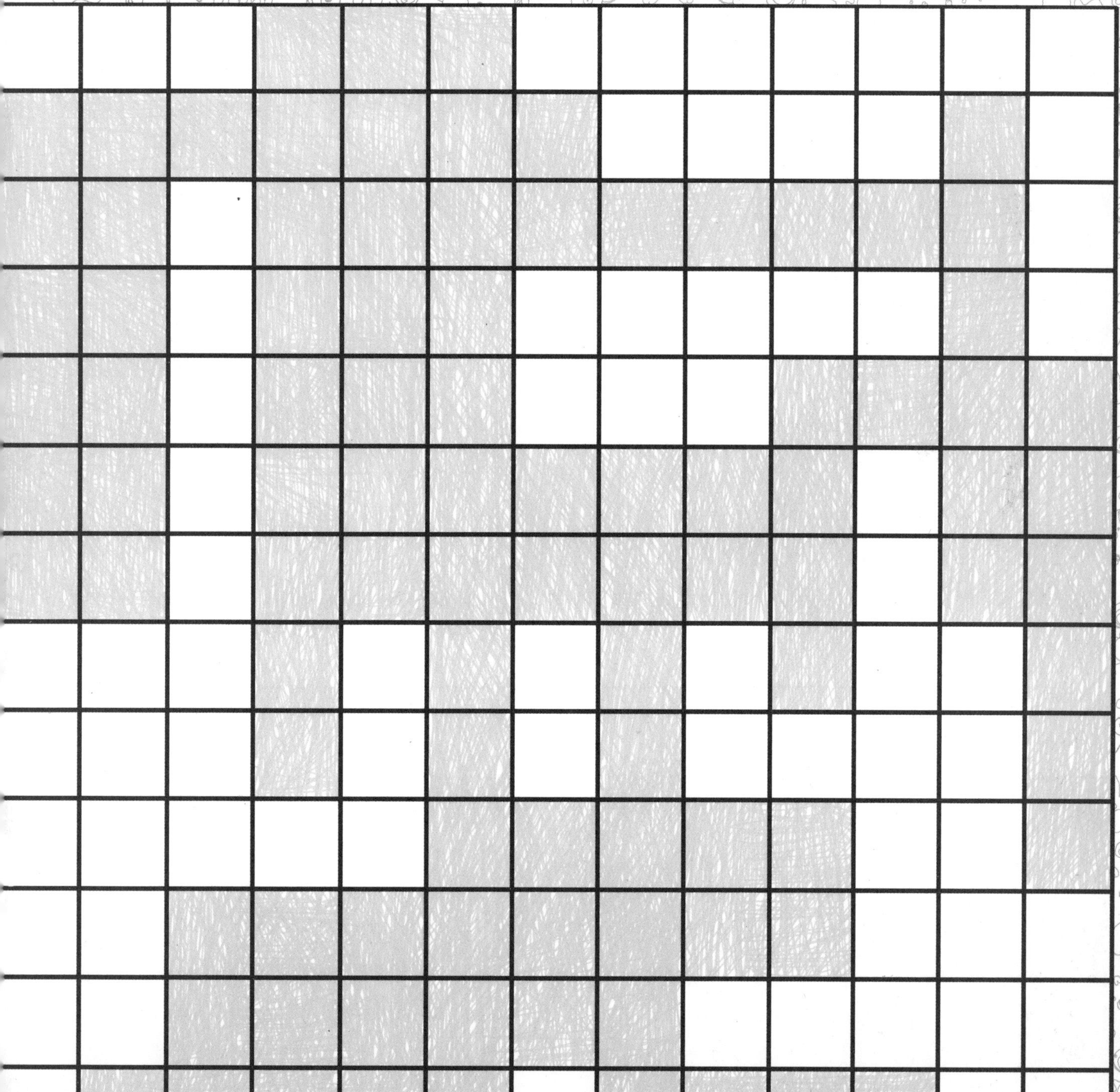

ZOMBIE CREEP

Pooey what a stinky creep!

Practice here...

ABCDEFGHIJ

KLMNOPQRS

TUVWXYZ !?

LET'S MAKE SOME
COOL STUFF

There are SO MANY things that you can make using your bubble writing and monster drawing skills. Here I'll show you a few to start you off. For this first activity: Cut the page in half (but leave it attached to the spine of the book!) and roll the right hand side of the page around a pencil. Now move the pencil from side to side to create a brilliant 2-page animation!
LIKE THIS!

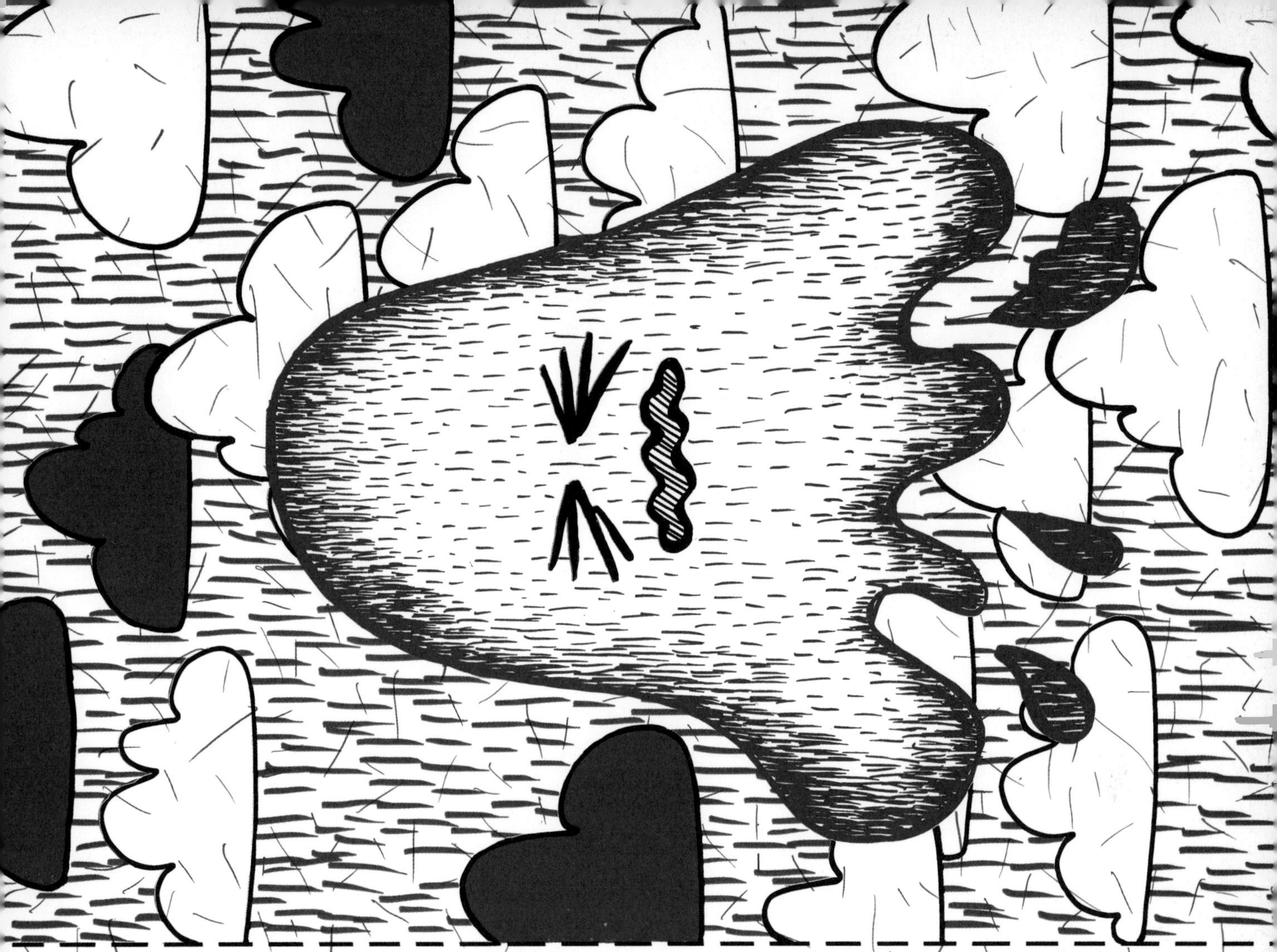

CUT HERE

MAKE YOUR OWN HERE

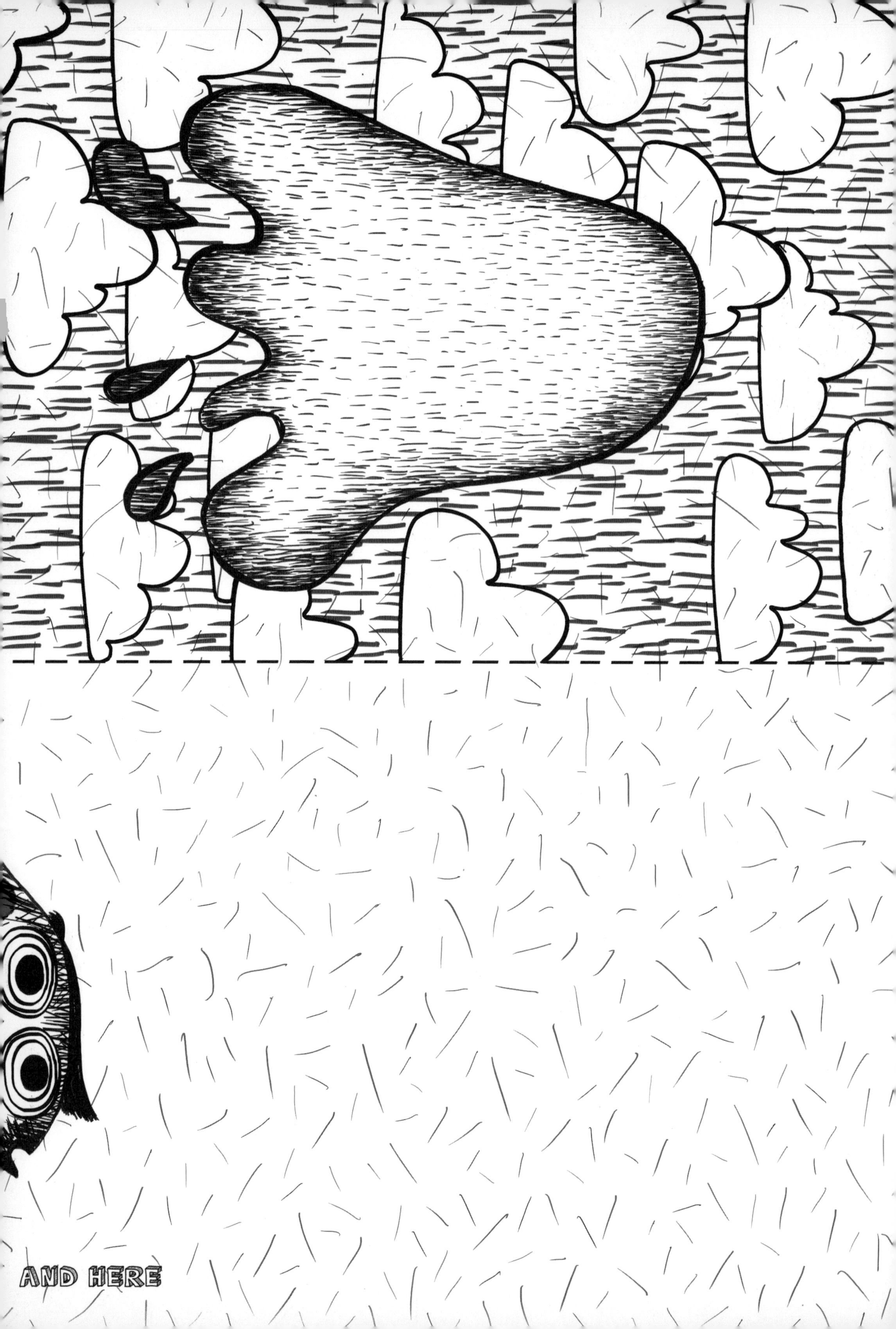
AND HERE

AND HERE

MAKE A FLICK BOOK

Grab a book of sticky notes or a small notebook. Now trace your character, working from the back page forward, moving it a little at a time. Now give it a title and front page.

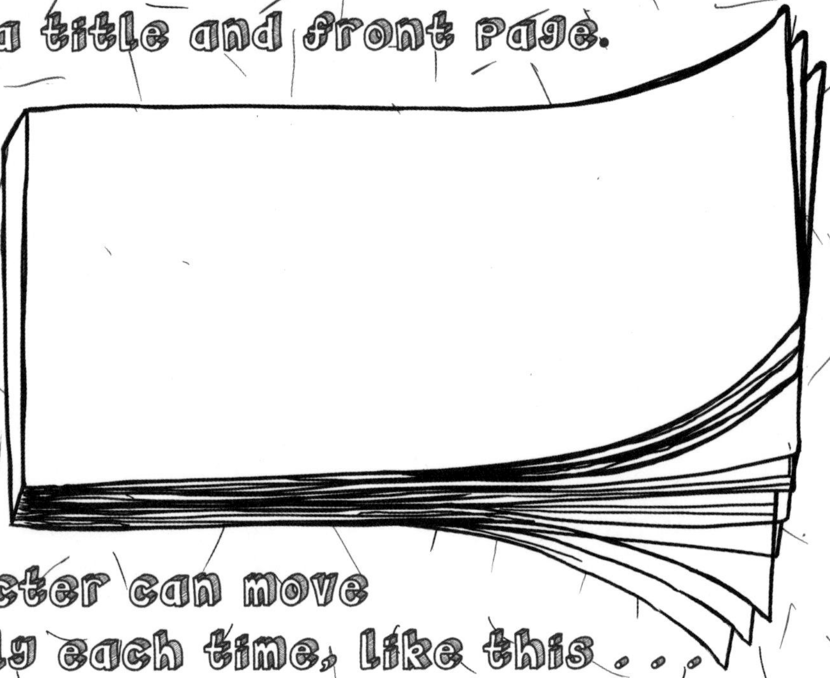

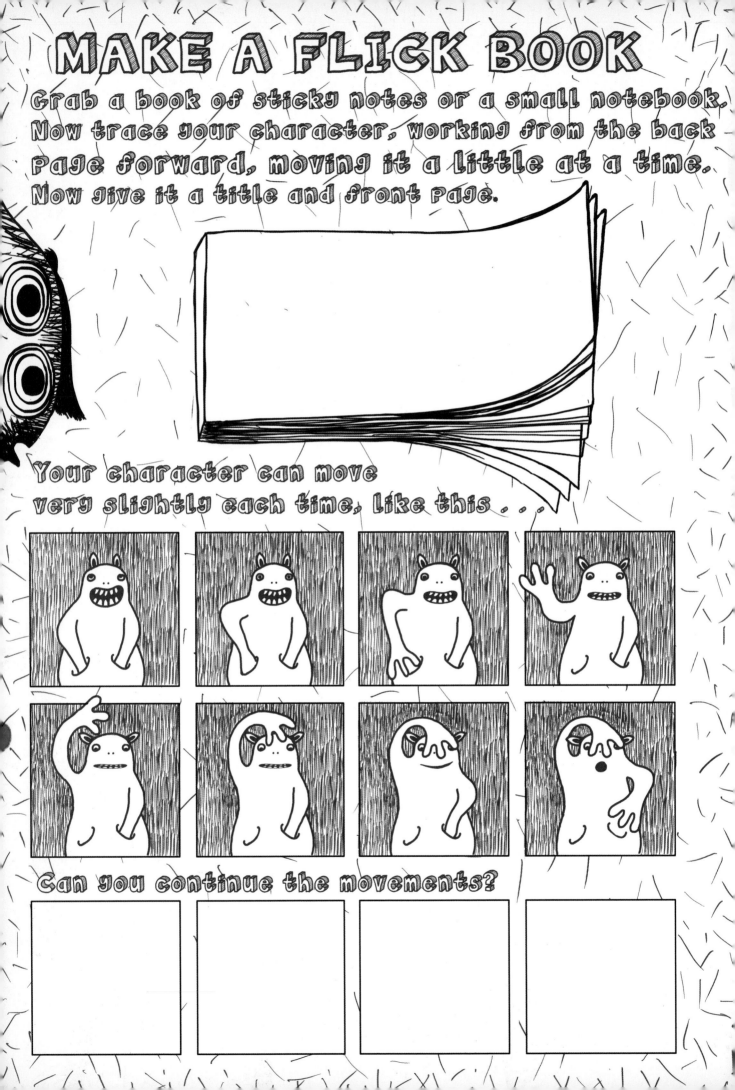

Your character can move very slightly each time, like this . . .

Can you continue the movements?

MAKE A POSTER
of something you
REALLY CARE about
Freedom for monsters

Monster pencil toppers

Design 'em, cut 'em out, and stick 'em round the top of your pencil

Make all of these ones zombies...

Cool !

MAKE YOUR OWN DOORHANGERS

THIS ROOM BELONGS TO THE AMAZING

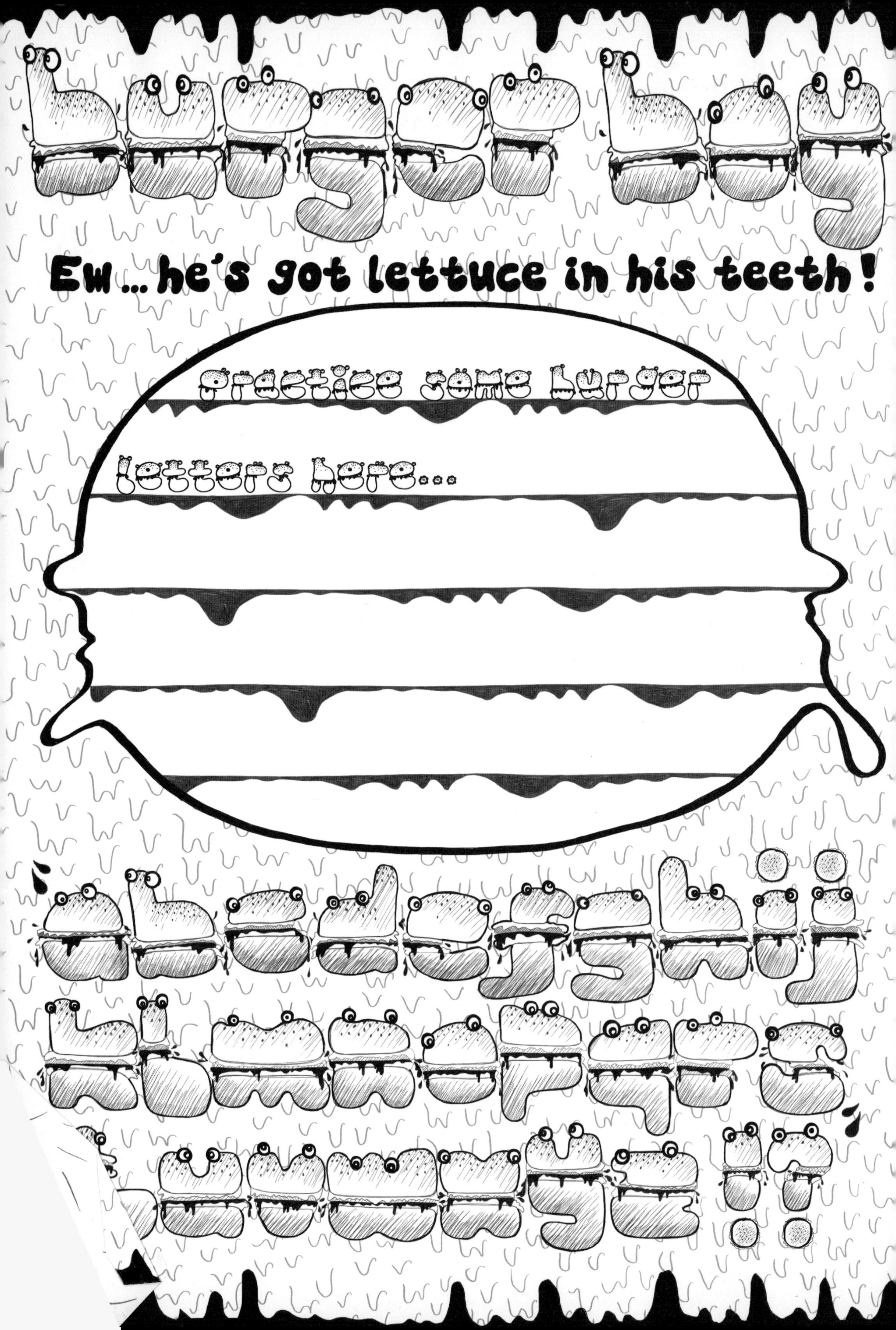
burger boy
Ew... he's got lettuce in his teeth!
practice some burger letters here...
abcdefghij
klmnopqrs
tuvwxyz!?

Let's write some
letters and notes

Texting, calling, and messaging is fun BUT there is nothing quite like getting something hand-written from someone who cares. ESPECIALLY if it's been bubble written! Here I'm going to show you how to make cool letters, postcards, notelets, secret notes, and cut-and-fold letters. Send them to your friends and family and just wait to see how happy it makes them. Bring it on!

Dear

From

write some cool love or friendship notes!

YOU ROCK

YOU ARE TOTES AMAZE

I HEART U

YOU MAKE MY HEART GO BOOM!

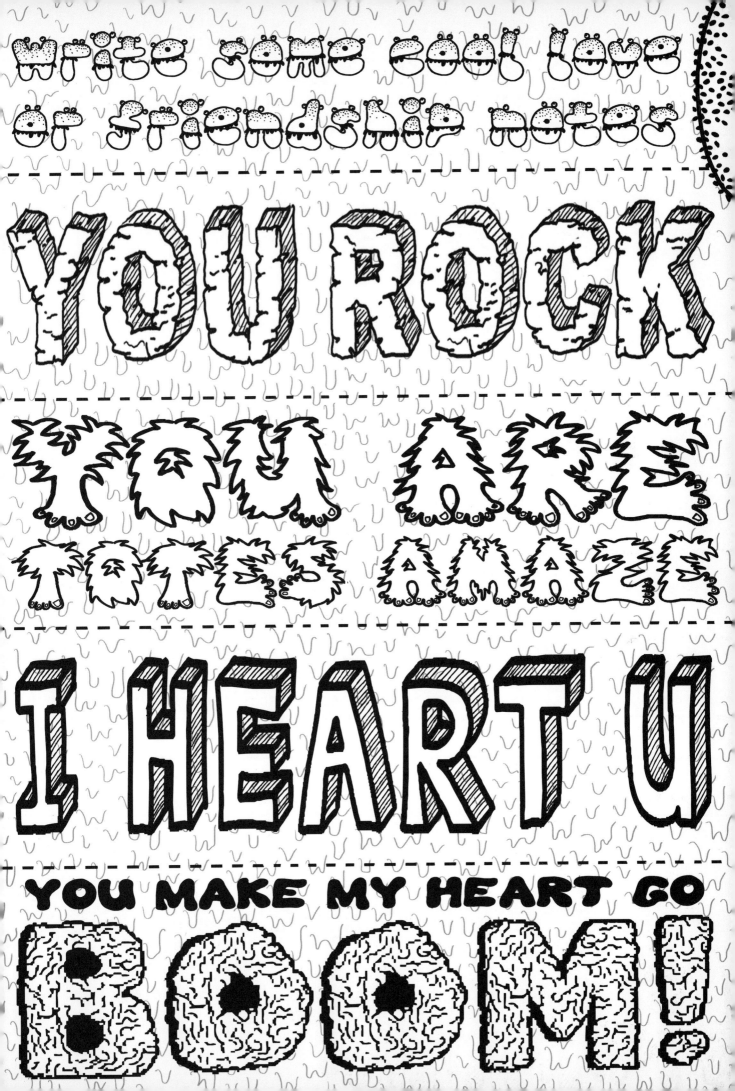

Add your own messages on the back here

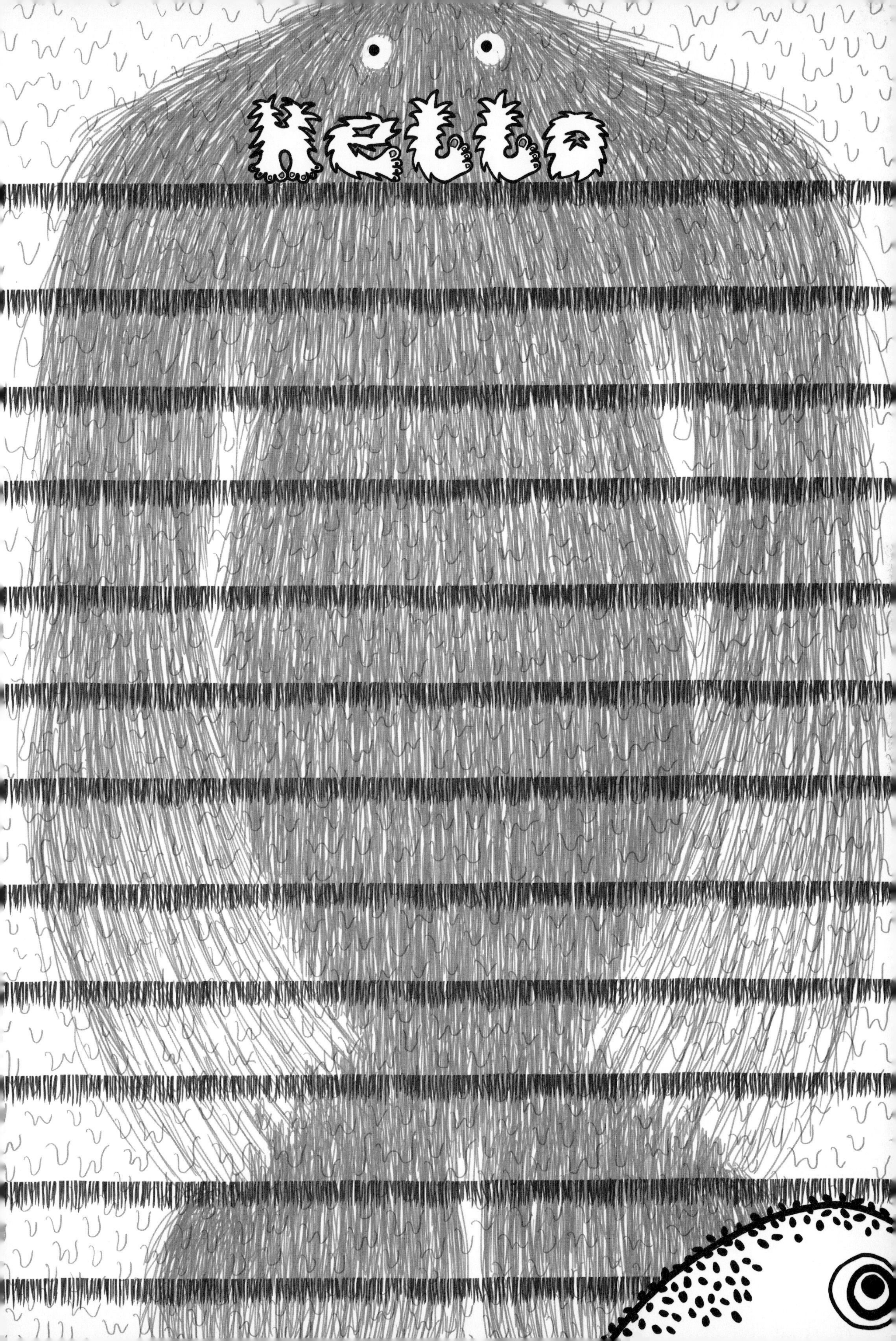
Hello

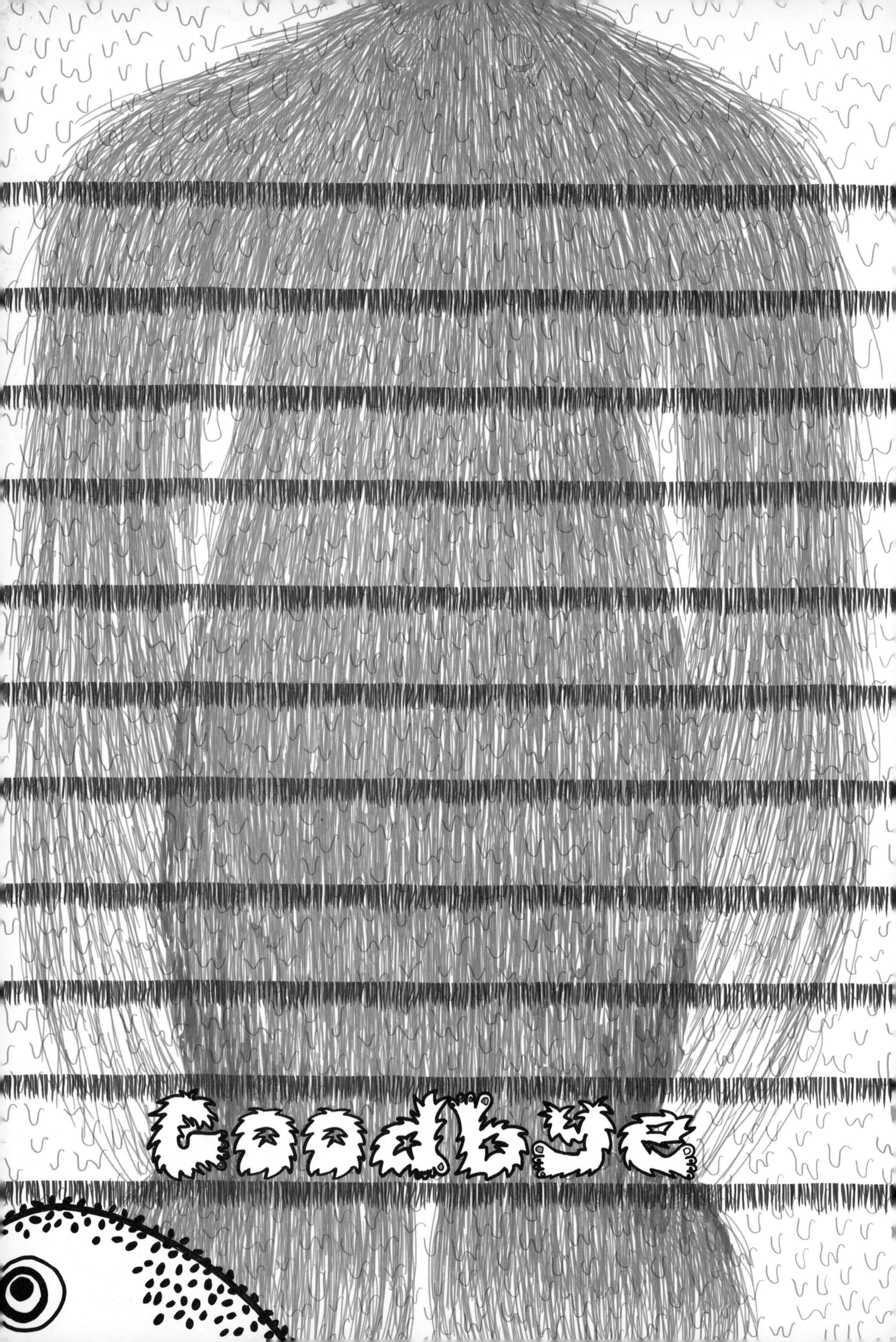
Goodbye

HEY YOU MONSTER
CHEEKY MONSTER

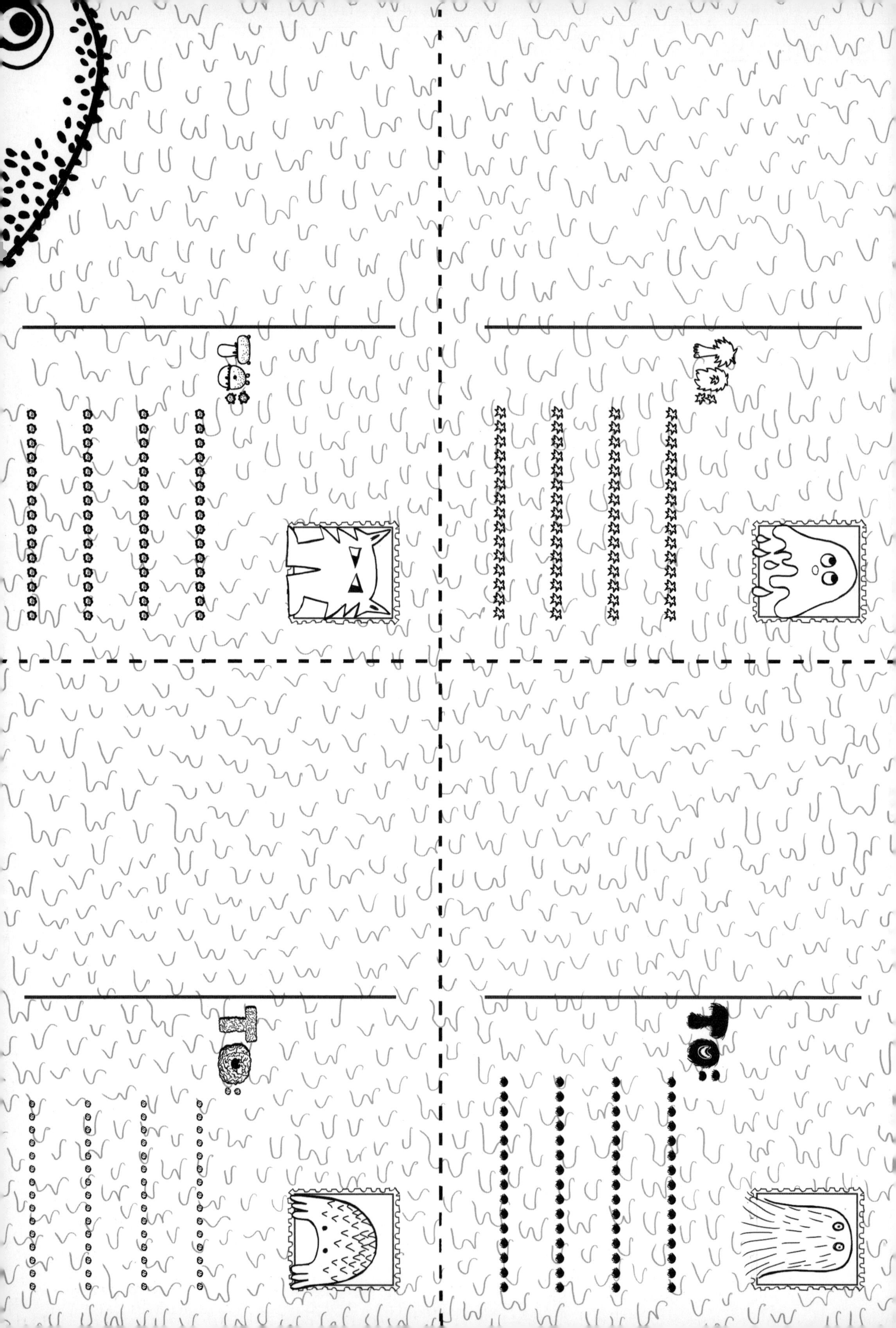

GLUE HERE AFTER FOLDING

GLUE HERE AFTER FOLDING

GLUE HERE AFTER FOLDING

Dear

From

A notelet from me to you

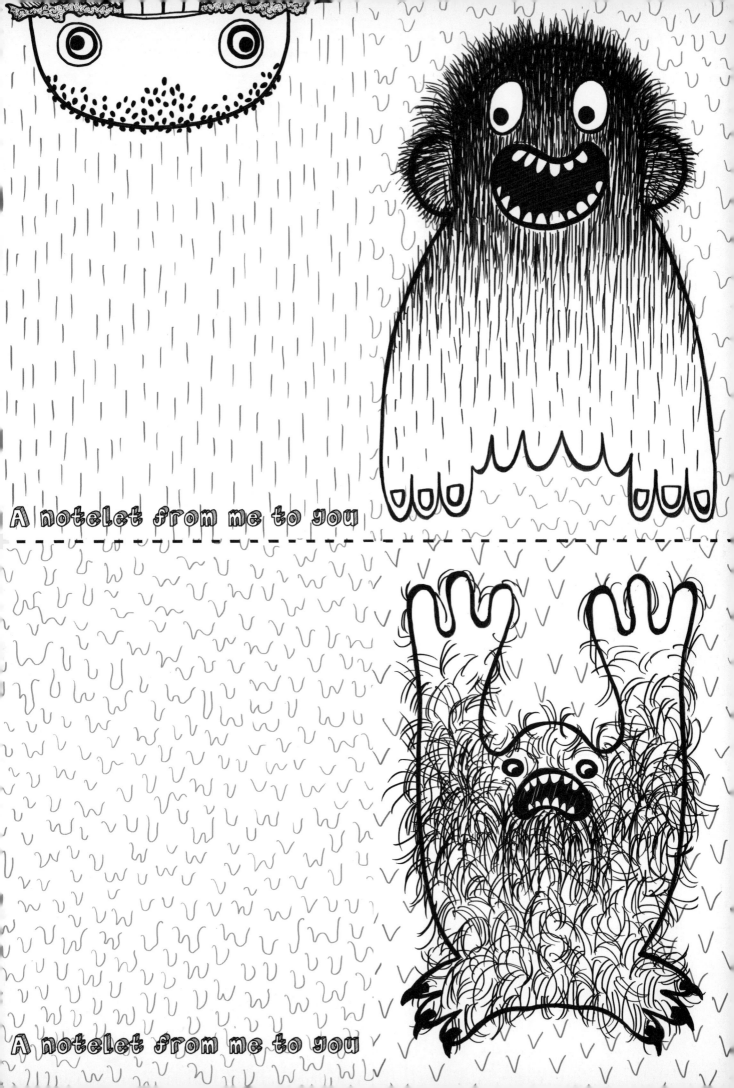

A notelet from me to you

Just a note to tell you
I've been thinking...

1

2

3

4

5

6

7

8

9

10

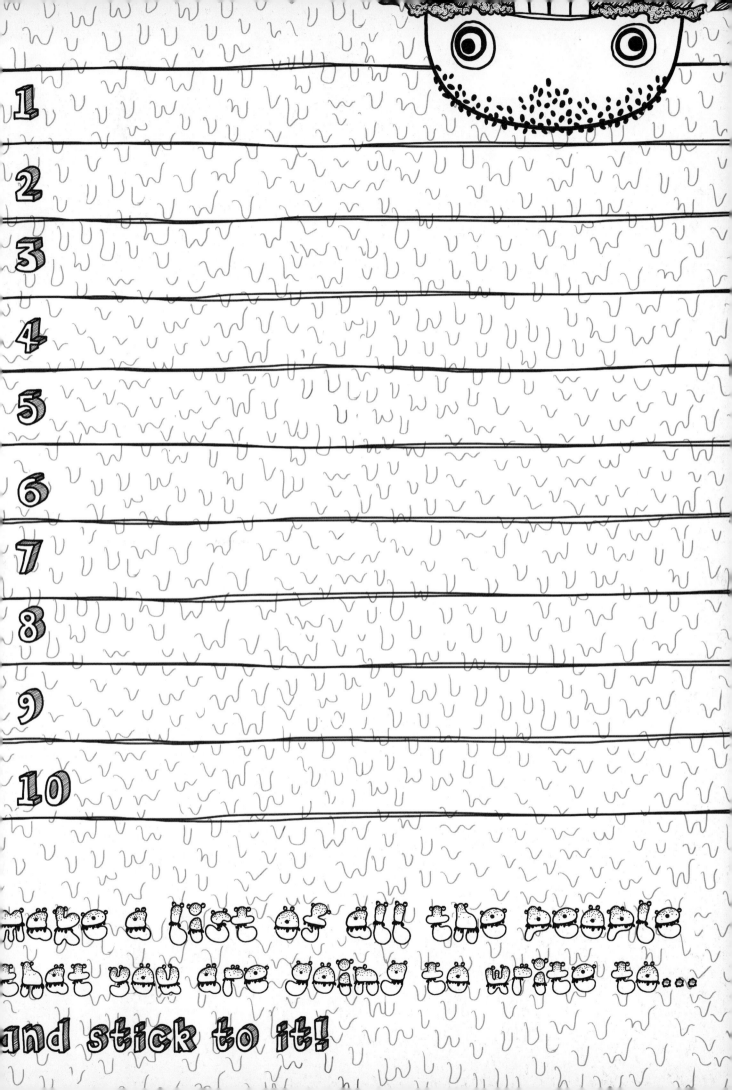

make a list of all the people that you are going to write to...

and stick to it!

crazy birdy numnums

Oy! What

Man, these monster birds are crazy!

PRACTICE YOUR CRAZIEST LETTERS HERE

"abcdefghij
klmnopqrs
tuvwxyz !?"

Let's make some stories and rhymes

Now we will look at all sorts of stories, rhymes, riddles, and poems. There are some great quotes and snippets to get you started here but the most important thing is for YOU to start writing yourself. It can be short or long, funny or sad, rhyming or ridiculous. Just start writing and see what comes!

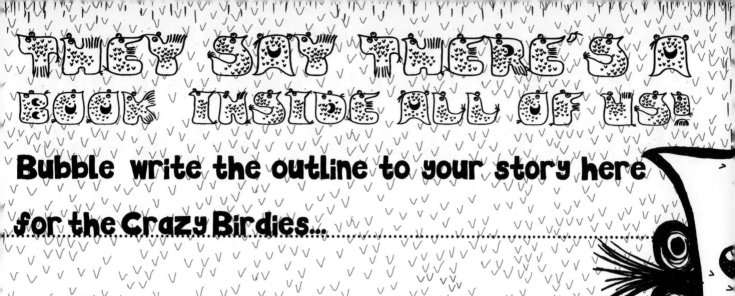

THEY SAY THERE'S A BOOK INSIDE ALL OF US!

Bubble write the outline to your story here for the Crazy Birdies...

CAN YOU WRITE THE CRAZY BIRDS A STORY AROUND THESE GREAT ROALD DAHL LINES?

The small girl smiles. One eyelid flickers. She pulls a pistol from her knickers.

Two rights don't equal a left.

I'd rather be fried alive and eaten by Mexicans.

DO IT IN BUBBLE WRITING OF COURSE!)

Don't gobblefunk around with words.

Lovely slugburgers. Delicious wormburgers.

And though he ate the pig quite fast, he carefully kept the tail til last.

CAN YOU FINISH THESE Edward Lear LIMERICKS?

There was an old person of Leeds,
Whose head was infested with ....,
She sat on a ....,
And ate gooseberry ....,
Which agreed with that person of ....

There was an old man in a boat,
Who said 'I'm afloat, I'm ....',
When they said 'No! You ....',
He was ready to ....,
That unhappy old man in a ....

There was an old man with a beard,
Who said 'It's just as I ....',
Two owls and a ....,
Four larks and a ....,
Have all built their nests in my ....

NOW YOU TRY YOUR OWN LIMERICKS

Here's the answers to the last page:

(No cheating now!)

fleas / stool / fool / Leeds

afloat / ain't / faint / boat

feared / hen / wren / beard

MAKE A MONSTER SHAPE WITH WORDS THAT DESCRIBE SOMEONE YOU KNOW (BE NICE!)

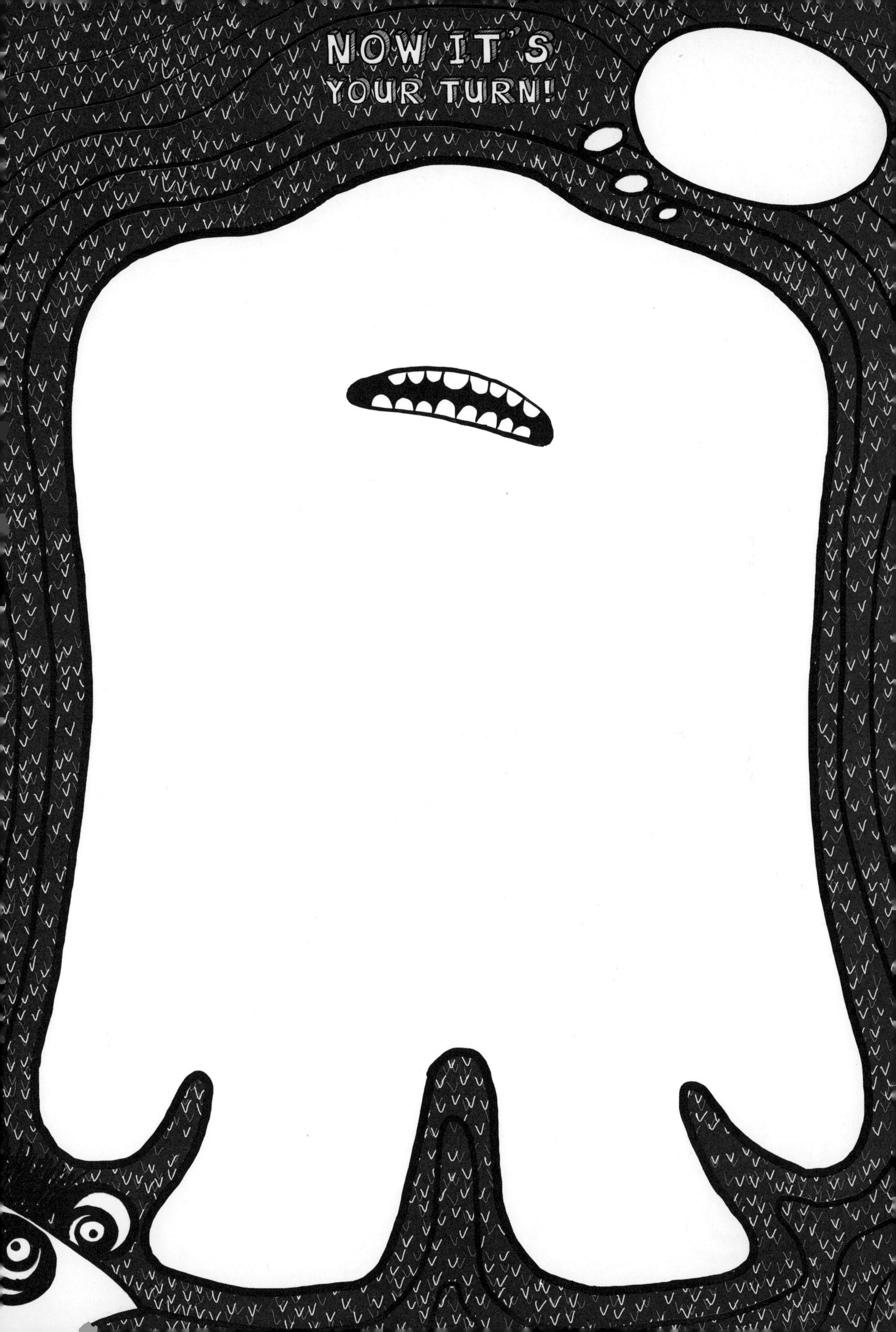
NOW IT'S
YOUR TURN!

MONSTER CONSEQUENCES

Find a friend, take it in turns writing just one line each and see what happens.

Suddenly I turned and saw

MONSTER CONSEQUENCES

Try and make this story completely different.

We crept into the dark attic

giggle monster

HE LAUGHS IN YOUR FACE! HOW RUDE.

Practice some giggles here...

abcdefghij
klmnopqrst
uvwxyz!?

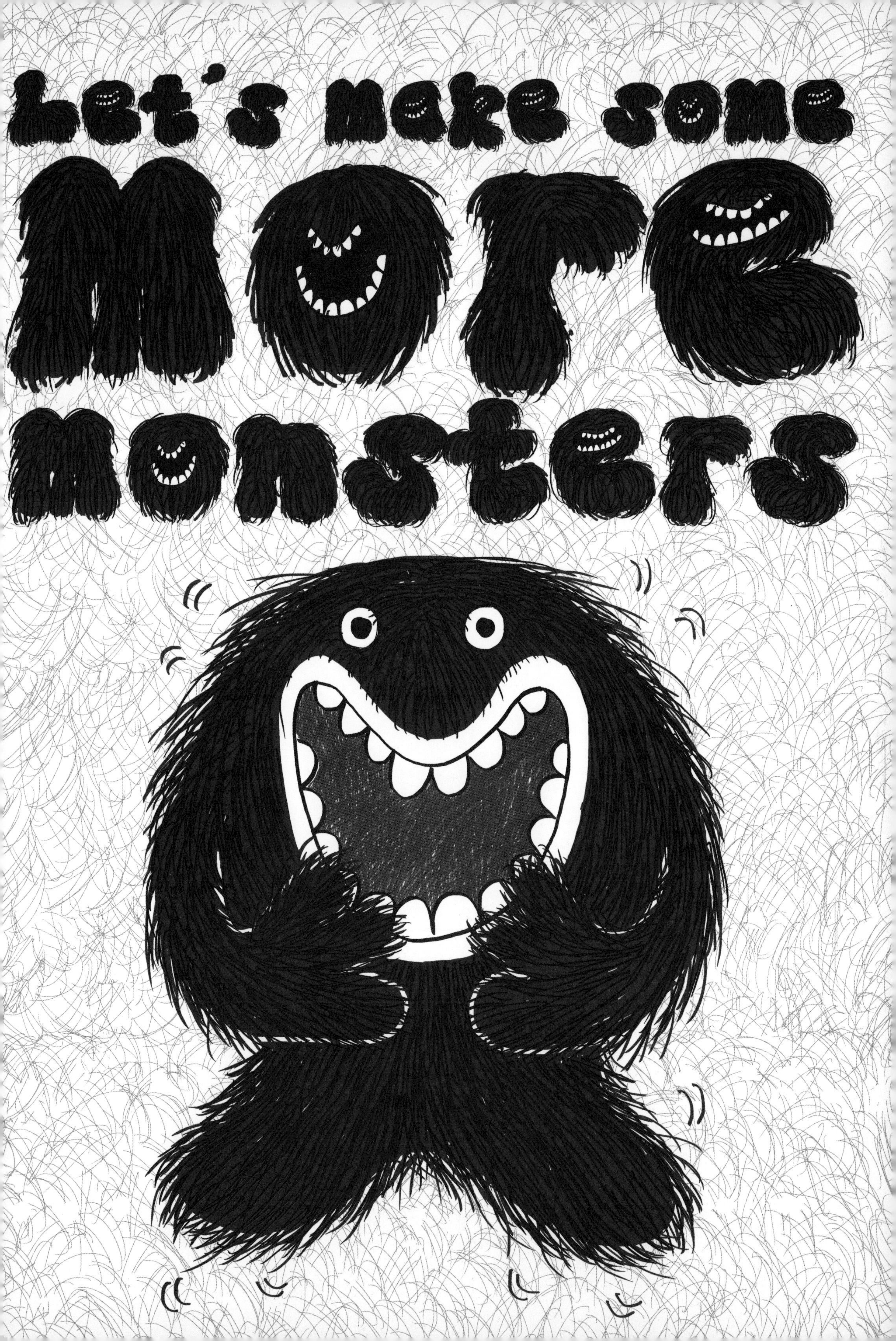
Let's make some
more
monsters

This is the last section of your Monster Bubble Writer Book! Yikes! So let's finish off where we started - by drawing MORE MONSTERS. By the time you finish this book you will either be a 'Monster-Drawing-Bubble-Writer Or a 'Bubble-Writing-Monster-Drawer'. Whichever one you become...enjoy the ride!

You can turn your friends into
friendly monsters
like this!
MONSTERS ARE THE FRIENDLIEST

Try and 'monster-up' some of your friends here (think about their faces, hair, smiles, style, and personalities to help)...

Psst ... It can make you feel really good to 'monster-up' some people you know who aren't so friendly too ...

Can you draw where this monster lives?

What do the monsters who live here look like?

Here are some more shapes to turn into monsters!

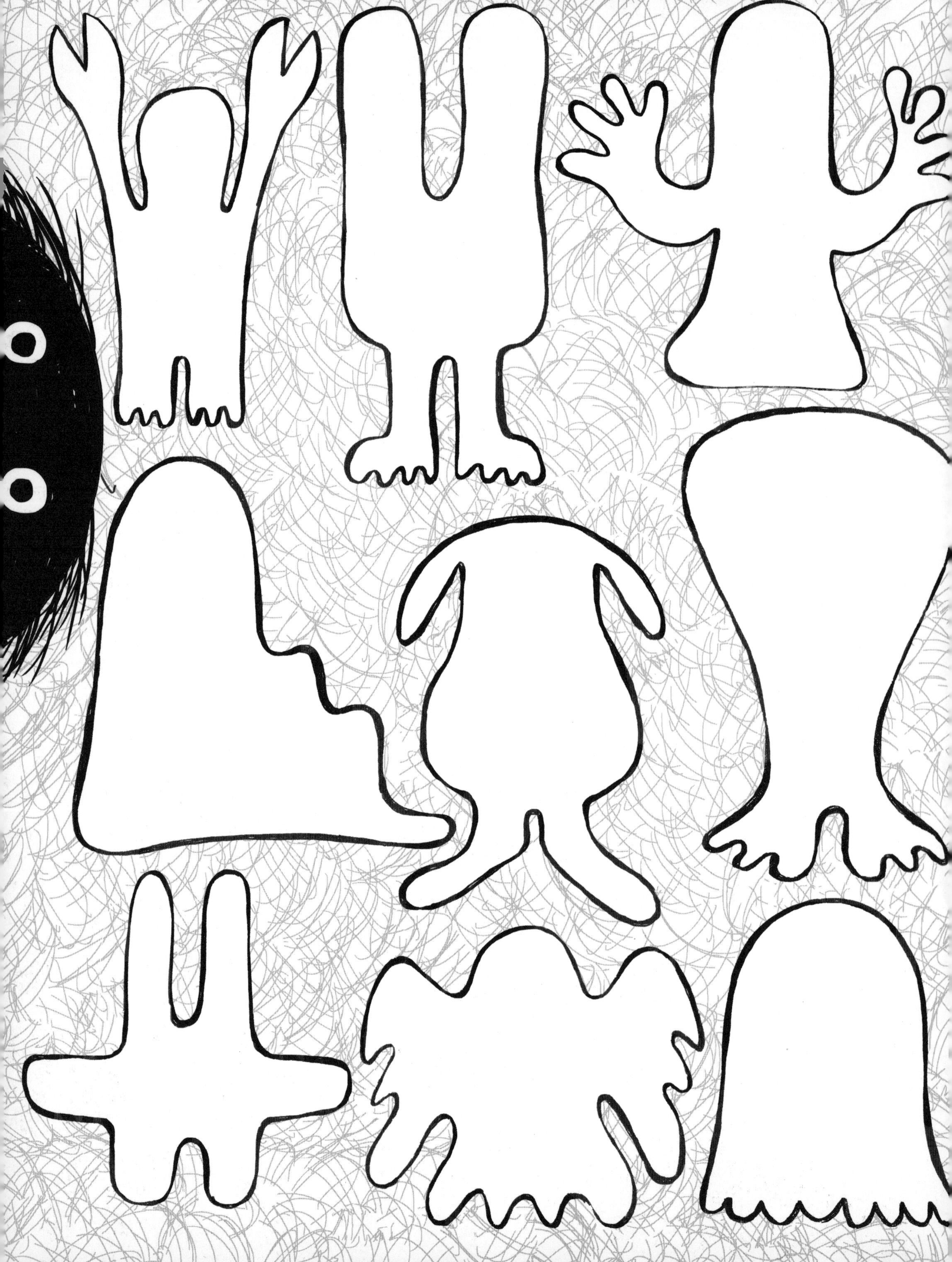

Here are some useful bits to help you make them!

Aargh!...Hair lice are like mini-monsters!

Draw lots of lice jumping on this poor dude's head...

Snot Monsters!

What the heck do they look like?

Draw some crawling out of this enormous honker...

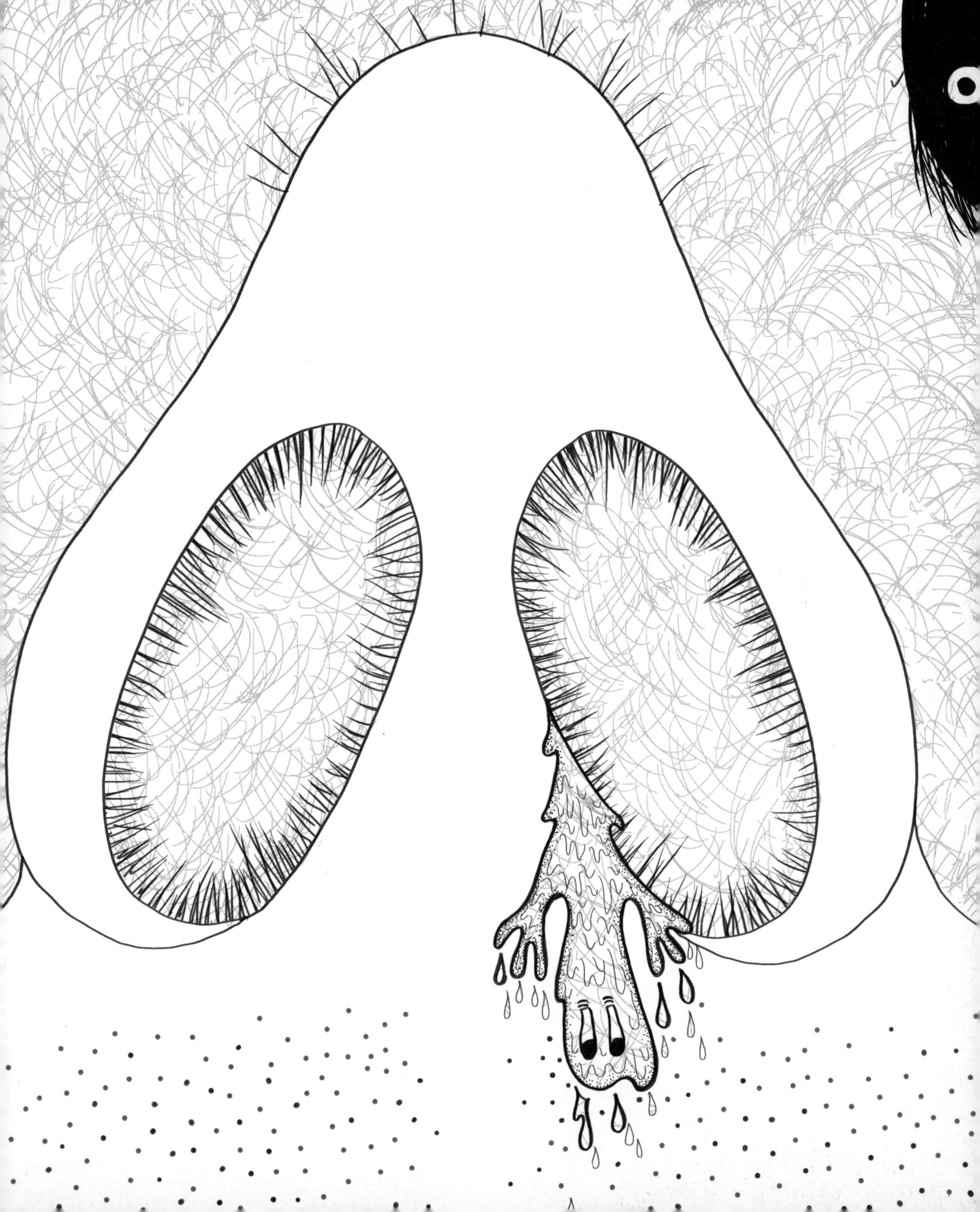

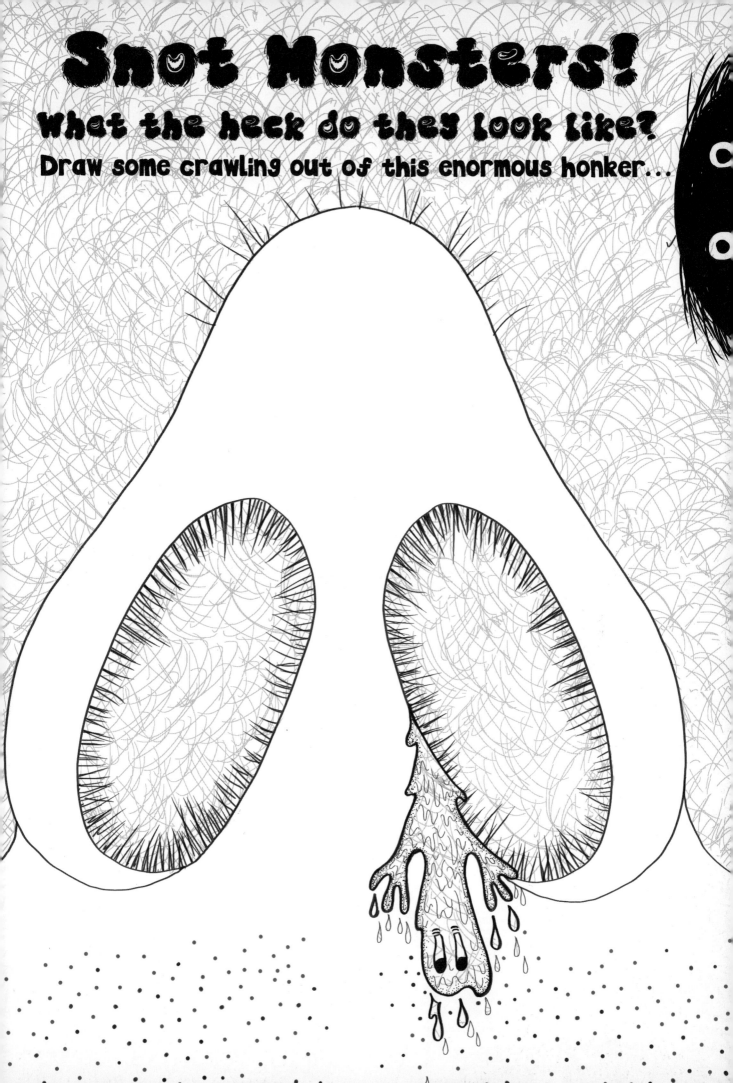

Draw the monsters that live under your bed

C' mon, I know you have some...

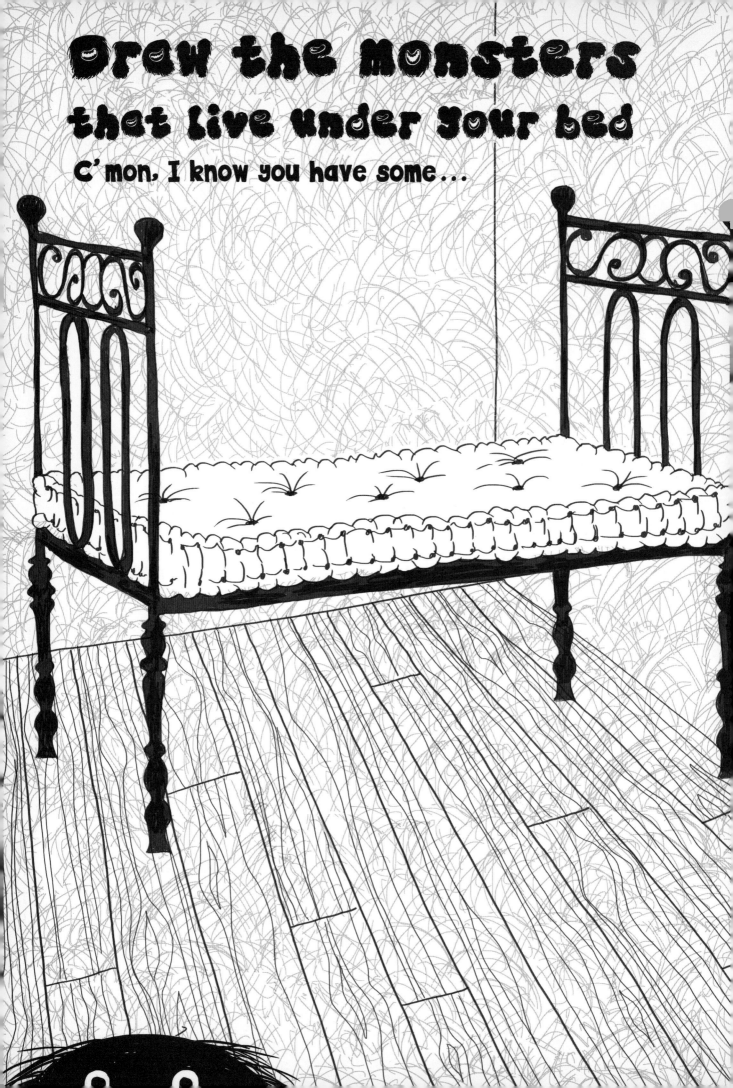

And the monsters in your wardrobe

Well, we all have at least one of these guys...

I am a monster - drawing bubble writer and my name is______________________________

Now make a monster of yourself!

I hope that you've enjoyed using this book as much as I've enjoyed making it!

I made all the alphabets (including this one) by hand-drawing them, and then uploading the drawn letters into a font generator so that they can then be typed out on a computer. Take a look at www.yourfonts.com for more info. It's quite easy and not too expensive.

There are loads of really great artists who draw monsters every day (probably) of their lives out there. There are too many to list but to see a few of the best, take a look at: Rachel Ortas, Jon Burgerman, Hayao Miyazaki, and David Horvath - and prepare to be completely blown away by their brilliance!

Thanks to the amazing authors whose wonderful words I used in the 'stories and rhymes' section.

www.facebook.com/thebubblewriter
www.bubblewriter.com

goodbye

THANKS FOR ALL YOUR HELP GUYS! Helen Rochester and Al (sorry I forgot you both last time!), Mick, Harvey, Bonnie, Theo, Rachel, Team Sam and Jess, and Karen.

MONSTER
THIS BOOK
HAS BEEN FINISHED BY
MONSTER